STRONGER MAN NATION
Biblical Manhood Series

PROVIDER WITH A FIELD TO WORK

Adam James

FARMER: Provider With A Field To Work

Copyright © 2023

Published by Grace City Publishing

All rights reserved. No part of this publication may be reproduced in any form, stored in a retrieval system, or transmitted in any form by any means—electronic, mechanical, photocopy, recording, or otherwise—without the prior permission of the publisher, except as provided by United States of America copyright law.

Editorial Team: Luke Ellington, Chief Editor; Karis McPherson, Art Director; and the Proofreading Team.

Printed in the United States of America.

To my dad, a first-generation Christian who worked hard to provide for his family.

To my fellow elders—you're the men I call first.

To the Stronger Men of Grace City Church, it's my privilege and joy to be among you.

You then, my **SON**, be strong in the grace that is in Christ Jesus. And the things you have heard me say in the presence of many witnesses entrust to reliable men who will also be qualified to teach others. Join with me in suffering, like a good **SOLDIER** of Christ Jesus. No one serving as a soldier gets entangled in civilian affairs, but rather tries to please his commanding officer. Similarly, anyone who competes as an **ATHLETE** does not receive the victor's crown except by competing according to the rules. The hardworking **FARMER** should be the first to receive a share of the crops. Reflect on what I am saying, for the Lord will give you insight into all this.

2 TIMOTHY 2:1-7

STRONGER MAN
N A T I O N

Welcome to Stronger Man Nation. We are more than a band of brothers. We're a movement of men committed to making good battle with our lives.

STRONGER MAN NATION
Biblical Manhood Series

Weekly devotions and discussion tools designed to build and strengthen men.

Ideal for individual or group study.

SOLDIER: PROTECTOR WITH A BATTLE TO FIGHT

FARMER: PROVIDER WITH A FIELD TO WORK

ATHLETE: LEADER WITH A CROWN TO WIN (Coming Summer 2023)

SON: LOVER WITH A FATHER TO PLEASE (Coming Fall 2023)

CONTENTS

Acknowledgments 1

Introduction 3

How To Use This Book 7

WEEK 1 STRONGER MEN LIVE LIKE FARMERS (2 Timothy 2:6) 8
  From A Stronger Man: Gary Polson

WEEK 2 BE FRUITFUL AND MULTIPLY (Genesis 1:27-28) 20
  From A Stronger Man: Galen Bierlink

WEEK 3 PROVIDE FOR YOUR HOUSEHOLD (1 Timothy 5:7-8) 32
  From A Stronger Man: Robb Myers

WEEK 4 STRONGER MEN ARE GIVERS NOT TAKERS (Ephesians 4:28) 42
  From A Stronger Man: Mike Taylor

WEEK 5 WORK WITH ALL YOUR HEART (Col. 3:23-24; 1 Cor. 15:58) 52
  From A Stronger Man: Shawn Ballard

WEEK 6 WARNING TO IDLE SLUGGARDS (Proverbs 24:30-34) 64
  From A Stronger Man: Tim Scott

WEEK 7 BREAK UP YOUR UNPLOWED GROUND (Hosea 10:12) 78
  From A Stronger Man: Max Polson

WEEK 8 ALL MEN REAP WHAT THEY SOW (Galatians 6:7-9) 88
  From A Stronger Man: Jim Newberry

WEEK 9 STRONGER MEN AND THE FOUR SOILS (Matthew 13:2-9) 100
  From A Stronger Man: Ray Schmitten

WEEK 10 VINE AND BRANCHES—TREE AND FRUIT (Jn. 15:1-8; Lk. 6:43-45) 114
  From A Stronger Man: Mark Stennes

WEEK 11 STRONGER MEN ARE PATIENT FARMERS (James 5:7-8) 124
  From A Stronger Man: Larry James

WEEK 12 ALL IN FOR THE LORD OF THE HARVEST (Luke 10:1-4) 136
  From A Stronger Man: Norris Williams

Additional Questions For Discussion 148

Ways To Practice Being A Farmer / Provider 150

ACKNOWLEDGMENTS

Pastor Josh McPherson, my friend and the best leader I know, thank you for leading the way and letting me come along. Your legacy of calling greatness out of men and leaders for Jesus' sake is only just beginning. Thank you, Jeff & Becky and the Weber family for providing a place for me to pray and write. Your friendship and generosity are refreshing and exemplary. Dad, Mom, Greg, Steve, Jeff, Ted, AR, Sam...and many others who prayed for me during the writing days—thank you! Once again, the talented and hard-working Luke Ellington and Karis McPherson, for your work to edit, layout, design, and bring this into fruition—thank you! To each of the stronger men and hard-working farmers who provided testimonies and exhortations—I knew the Lord would give you the words, and He did—thank you! My Friday AM Stronger Men group, you're a constant source of encouragement and strength—thank you! To all the hard-working farmers of NCW and Eastern Washington, in particular, from Waterville to Spokane, Ellensburg to Canada, the Wenatchee and Yakima valleys, and all those "B" school farm towns, if you know, you know. And of course, the James Gang: My wife, Erin, my greatest encourager, supporter, and the most beautiful editing eyes; Grace, Ben, Noelle, and Sam, you give me my greatest opportunities to be a stronger man in action, and I love being your dad!

INTRODUCTION

God made men to be farmers.

Workers. Producers. Providers.

To every man reading this: *you have a field to work and a harvest to reap.*

There's just something about a man and dirt, isn't there?

We see it in young boys. Boys and dirt. It's as natural as peanut butter and jelly or pancakes and syrup.

It's because God made men from dirt. He formed the first man, Adam, from the dust of the ground. And to the dirt, we all eventually return. In the meantime, we have work to do. And that's a good thing.

God gives us a field to work and a harvest to reap. Not just in the physical dirt but in the holy calling of our lives, relationships, vocations, and character.

There's a field in your family, in your job, at your school, in your neighborhood, through your business, and in your church. There's a field in your city, state, and nation. There's a field and a harvest in your generation and in your own soul.

We are called to be fruitful men, productive men, hardworking men. Men with the heart of a provider and an eye toward the harvest.

Does that overwhelm you? It could. There's a lot of work to do, but don't let it take you off the field. Instead, let it motivate you to discover your part and embrace it fully. Stronger men lean into the plow!

Stronger men—men being made new by Jesus—cause the people and things around them to flourish and thrive.

The call of God on men to be Farmers is not a burden but a blessing. It's a privilege and responsibility that is filled with soul-satisfying reward.

There's good work to do! Great purpose to live into. Amazing harvest to work for and enjoy.

These are not days to sit on our hands, stare at screens, kick the dirt, and curse the darkness. These are not days to complain about the way things are.

These are days to look ahead, make a plan, and do something about it.

Men are wired to discover and live with purpose. The good news is that life is not meaningless. As the ultimate Farmer, Worker, and Creator, God made men with dignity, value, and yes, purpose.

In the beginning, God made man from the dust of the ground. He blessed him and gave him work to do. He put him in a garden and told him to work it and take care of it. He commanded him to be fruitful and multiply, to fill the earth and subdue it.

Our first father, Adam, failed in his work, disobeyed God, and the curse fell upon us as a result. Now, work is often hard and painful. The ground fights back. Thorns and weeds grow. Pests abound. Moths and rust destroy. Thieves break in. Wolves attack. Winter hits hard.

You now live and work in "painful toil." "By the sweat of your brow."

When it comes to work: God gave it. We broke it. Jesus redeems it.

The curse of sin distorts men's relationship with work in two primary ways.

On one hand, men are prone to be lazy and work too little. To quit working. To seek a life of ease, comfort, and pleasure. All you have to do is look around, and if you're honest, within. Men often look for shortcuts, do the absolute minimum necessary, hit snooze, roll over, look for handouts, play stupid games, and live off the hard work of others. As a result, many men are weak, soft, dependent, lazy, sluggards, and whiners. It's a massive problem and a drag on society, and women and children (and the rest of us) pay the price. There is no shortage of lazy men.

On the other hand, many men work too much. They worship their work, never stop burning the candle at both ends, waste their resources on trivial things, neglect their families, and end up being crushed or consumed by their work. Men can find a false sense of worth and identity from their work, which leaves them utterly disoriented when they aren't working. Many still end up destroying themselves and others. The loss of work exposes a void that must still be filled. How many men throw themselves at the idol or temple of work? They are unable to build thriving relationships and eventually run themselves, or those around them, into the ground. There is no shortage of men in bondage to work.

In both ways, our sin has broken our relationship with work because our sin has broken us. Broken men, in turn, break things and people.

Jesus came to undo the curse and do the work we couldn't. He came to redeem work and redeem men to do good work as image-bearers of God. He's the Second Adam, the Better Man—the Stronger Man—who succeeded where the first failed. Men can be redeemed by Jesus to become the farmers, workers, and providers they were intended to be.

Men were made from the ground and to the ground we will all return. Ashes to ashes and dust to dust. Lord willing, we'll be good and tired, having lived a life of stronger manhood, of noble work, with a great harvest that honors the God who made us.

There are just two options for what happens at that moment our bodies return to the ground and our souls pass on into eternity. We will hear one of two things:

"*Well done, good & faithful servant.*" Or, "*Away from Me, I never knew you.*" The stakes are that high.

The Apostle Paul wrote his final letter—his second letter to his spiritual son and pastoral protégé, Timothy—to pass the baton of the work of God to the next generation of men. Who would, in turn, pass it on to the next generation. And those men to the next.

At the center of Paul's strategy—God's strategy—is raising up more men. More Farmers. Stronger men. Strong in the grace of God. The call was for Timothy himself to **become** a stronger, godly man and to pass on what he had been given to **build** up another generation who would in turn love, lead, and **bless** women and children.

Become. Build. Bless. That's the three-pronged call of God for men. Become stronger men who build stronger men who bless women, children, and the Church.

God's great mission—the redemption and salvation of the world—requires a man-making mission.

All through the Scriptures and the story of God, men are called to be protectors, providers, leaders, and lovers. These roles are seen in the four images of the soldier, farmer, athlete and son. Taken right from 2 Timothy chapter 2, these images carry much of the essence of true and noble manhood.

In these four images, there is a mountain of manhood to be explored. There is a lifetime of growth and maturity and responsibility to receive. These masculine images have carried the ethos of true manhood for millennia.

They are not four different men; they are to be woven into one image. Four parts of one man who finds his ultimate model and perfect example in the person of Jesus Christ.

These four man-types are a picture of the divine design of noble manhood, and they come with a living promise.

2 Timothy 2:7
Reflect on what I am saying, for the Lord will give you insight into all this.

We'd be wise to reflect on them afresh in our day and rediscover those spiritual insights.

You hold in your hands the second book in a series of 4 that unpack each of these identities for men through the pages of Scripture, in 12 weekly chapters. Each chapter is designed to be worked through on your own, with other men, or with your own sons. The 4-book series provides a unique, one-year curriculum designed to help men become stronger men who build stronger men.

The need arises in every generation. The fields are as ripe for harvest as they've ever been. It's our turn to answer the call. Let's dig in!

HOW TO USE THIS BOOK

We're so excited for you to get started and dive in, on your own or with your men's group. Scan the QR code below to watch a short tutorial on how to get the most out of your study.

WEEK 1

STRONGER MEN LIVE LIKE FARMERS

THE HARDWORKING FARMER

should be the first to receive
a share of the crops.

2 TIMOTHY 2:6

1 Stronger men, like farmers, get up and get after it. Stronger men work hard.

If you want to be a real man, you must learn to work hard. Day in and day out.

Just like "the hardworking farmer."

If you've ever seen it or done it, you know that good farming is flat out hard work.

I grew up in North Central Washington. Farming country. Fruit, wheat, cattle, timber. My first job was in an apple orchard fixing sprinklers. I was 13 years old. The mowers and sprayers would often run over a sprinkler and break the pipes.

My friend, whose parents owned a good bit of orchard, and I spent an entire summer walking the rows of trees, finding the puddles of water or spurting geysers of broken pipes. We'd shut off the water, dig down around the pipe, clean it, dry it, cut it, glue on the coupling, glue on a new section of pipe, and put the sprinkler head back on. Row after row. Sprinkler after sprinkler. All summer.

The next year, it was summer pruning. We took pruning shears, drove around on motorbikes, and pruned the suckers growing up in the middle of trees, which were sucking precious nutrients from the tree—with no fruit to show. Row after row. Tree after tree. Day after day.

WEEK ONE

Every summer in my youth, I worked in the orchards and down at the packing sheds. Thinning apples, building bins, painting shed doors, stacking pallets, tying down boxes with twine, driving all over the valley from orchard block to orchard block carrying out various tasks. I even got to drive some forklift down at the shed, on occasion.

Can you imagine the list of things that need to get done to successfully grow fruit at scale? Let alone all the other types of farming? It's an incredible amount of work. Most of us can barely keep our grass mowed and the weeds out of our own yards.

Looking back, it was an awesome way to grow up and a great way to learn to work hard. Even as a young man, I knew that I barely knew the half of it. Those owners and workers who make their living by farming are a special breed. I have huge respect for farmers. It truly is a sacred way of life, and doing it well and doing it right really does require hard work.

But don't just take my word for it. God, Himself, uses farmers as a prototype example of hard work. Let's take His Word for it!

The whole story of the Bible, in fact, starts with a man with a lot of work to do in a garden.

In his final instruction to Timothy, after charging him with the task of entrusting the gospel to reliable men who will, in turn, pass it on to others (2 Timothy 2:2), the Apostle Paul likened Christian life and leadership to that of being a soldier, an athlete, and a farmer.

As men, we are called to be like farmers. And like farmers, we are called to be hard workers.

Are you giving yourself fully to the things the LORD has given you to do in this season of your life? Are you working hard in your current roles?

2. Stronger men, like farmers, know their role and know their limits—they do their job and trust God to do His.

Farming and faith go hand in hand. Farmers do their work in faith. They trust that God's creative power and created order will bring about the result they are after. There is so much that is out of their control.

==When you truly believe that God is ultimately in control of the outcome, it does several powerful things in your life.==

It frees you to truly work hard.
This may seem counter intuitive. If God is in control, why try? But that's not actually how it works.

Think about it. Very few things thwart your energy or output like a lack of confidence. When you're unsure of what you're doing, why you're doing it, or if it will even matter in the end, you're not exactly motivated to give it your best.

Confidence is a secret weapon—not over-confidence. That's a liability. True, appropriate confidence is a contagious, compelling, propelling quality in a man, in a worker.

What is confidence and where does it come from? At its root, the word "confidence" is 'con' (with) + 'fide' (faith). Confidence means "with faith."

When you have faith in what you're doing, why you're doing it, and the difference you're making, you give it your all. How much more should our faith in God and in His promises propel us to give our best? That's exactly what happens. When we trust His Word and truly believe what He says, we are free to truly work hard, harder and happier than we've ever worked before, and for far better reasons!

==When we trust that God is in control of the outcome, we are free to give it our all, knowing our all is being placed in the hands of God and will not be in vain. Regardless of the outcome we do or don't see, we can work hard, by faith in the God of the invisible, the God of the impossible, the God of the eternal. Nothing put in His hands gets wasted. In fact, usually it gets transformed and multiplied!==

When you truly believe that God is in control of the outcome, it frees you to stop and call it a day.

At some point, the day's work comes to an end. Have you ever felt like or even said, "my work never stops." If that's you as you read this, that's a problem. If you can't shut it off or shut it down for a night, or for a day, something's outta whack. And eventually, you'll hit a wall and pay a price. As will those around you.

If you can't take a break, or if you have a hard time ever sitting still and resting, it most likely means that you don't actually believe that God is in control and you're carrying it all on your shoulders. Or you want some kind of credit. Either way, it is actually a form of pride. If it's not crushing you yet, it will.

When you truly believe that God is in control of the outcome, you freely give Him all the glory for the results.

To be a stronger man is to work hard—all the while knowing that your role and your power is actually very limited—and ultimately

WEEK ONE

dependent on God's blessing and protection.

==Whatever harvest you are after, you must work hard, pouring yourself out, then rest well in faith, knowing beyond the shadow of a doubt that God is still working while you're resting and that He alone deserves all the credit for whatever comes to fruition.==

Psalm 127:1 says, "*Unless the LORD builds the house, its builders labor in vain. Unless the LORD watches over the city, the watchmen stand guard in vain.*"

When men think they are the "it" factor, the X factor—there is trouble on the horizon. It ain't you, pal. Apart from God, you can do nothing.

We may plow, plant, and water...but only God makes it grow.

The work of your hands is nothing without the blessing of God.

Are you working hard, resting well, and clear in your heart and mind who gets all the glory?

3 Stronger men, like farmers, cultivate fruitfulness in the people and tasks under their care and influence.

Before I sat down to write this today, I got a text from a farmer friend who I had asked to be praying for me and for this book you're now holding.

It said, "The hardworking farmer works diligently with one thing on his mind. THE HARVEST."

For me, the book you now hold *is* the harvest of his prayers and the work of writing. But even this tool is intended for a greater harvest of encouraging and impacting you. The real harvest will hopefully be in your mind, heart, and life. And even beyond that in the lives of those YOU bless and impact.

Paul said to Timothy, "The hardworking farmer should be the first to receive a share of the crops."

Never lose sight of the joy of the harvest! Everything we do is for the goal of the harvest.

God doesn't just call us to farm, he commands us to be fruitful. Harvest is the goal. Fruit is the aim.

When you work hard, in faith, there's nothing sweeter than a taste of the fruit.

Stronger men produce good fruit. What kind of fruit? The Fruit of the Spirit (Galatians 5:22-23). The fruit of godliness. The fruit of productivity and creativity. The fruit of health and growth. The fruit of order instead of chaos. The fruit of humility instead of arrogance. The fruit of repentance instead of denial. The fruit of provision for your family.

Jesus said, "You'll know a tree by its fruit."

One time Jesus cursed a fig tree and it withered and died—why did He curse it? Because it was the season for figs but the tree didn't have any fruit. No fruit? What's the point? If it's not bearing fruit, it gets cut down and thrown in the fire.

Some of you probably remember the Wendy's commercial and marketing slogan, "Where's the beef?" Jesus is asking, "Where's the fruit?"

Hard work. Faith. Fruit. That's the life of a farmer. That's the life of a stronger man.

WEEK ONE

> "Cultivators of the earth are the most valuable citizens. They are the most vigorous, the most independent, the most virtuous, and they are tied to their country and wedded to its liberty and interests by the most lasting bonds."
>
> — Thomas Jefferson

FARMER

FROM A STRONGER MAN

I've been married for 37 years, and my wife and I have been blessed with 3 children and 1 grandchild, so far. I grew up with a knowledge of the Lord, but it wasn't until I had children of my own that I would say I have really walked with Jesus. My family has been farming wheat in Douglas County for 70 years. I have farmed full-time for the past 27 years and farmed as a second job for the 11 years prior. We farm 7,800 acres of dryland wheat and produce roughly 200,000 bushels per year.

As a farmer, God has shown me time and time again His faithfulness in providing for our needs. Even in the lean, years He has provided. What I love about farming is that we really realize that our efforts to make things happen can only go so far—so much is totally out of our control—such as the moisture we get (as we don't irrigate) and the price we sell for (which is totally out of our hands). **As men, we want to just forge ahead and take care of things, but all we can do as a farmer is prepare the soil, plant the seed, and pray for God to do the rest.**

As husbands, we need the farmer mentality of cultivating. A farmer cultivates the soil to give the seed a good foundation, yet as he cultivates it he is removing any weeds that come to steal precious moisture in the soil. As husbands, we have to cultivate a relationship with our wife, caring for her needs and keeping our love for her strong, cultivating our heart with God's word to make sure any weeds don't get started that would damage our marriage.

A farmer's mentality is also needed for raising our children. Cultivating their hearts as young children and fertilizing them with love and tenderness—planting the seed of God's Word in their hearts. I see this as being valuable so that when they are older and making their own decisions—when they face a period of darkness and hard times—they will draw on God's Word and truth. This is like farming—we take care of the soil, preparing it all spring and summer for planting. We plant the seed and watch it come up in the fall and begin to grow into a beautiful crop. Then winter comes, snow covers the wheat, and it is like a period of darkness. If the winter is short, it will come out looking just as beautiful as when the snow fell. But if the period of darkness is long and hard, it will look sick and dead when the snow leaves. But like a heart that God's Word has been planted into, it will begin to grow when the light has warmed it, calling it out of the state of despair. Such is the light of Christ when He shines on your heart and you come out from the darkness.

Gary, 63

REFLECT & DISCUSS

1. What is your biggest takeaway from this chapter?

_____
_____
_____

2. What was your first job? When did you truly learn the value of hard work?

_____
_____
_____

3. In what ways do you need to grow as a Farmer/Provider?

_____
_____
_____

4. What's the hardest thing about your current job/work?

_____
_____
_____

5. Where does "faith" come in to the equation in your work? What do you need to trust God for?

6. Where can you see some good fruit currently in your life and relationships? In those around you, under your influence/leadership?

7. What's the greatest threat to your Harvest right now?

TAKE ACTION

- Identify one "hard" thing that you've been putting off. Take action on it this week.

- Make a list of the most important relationships in your life. Identify one way you can serve them or encourage them practically or tangibly. Pick 3-4 to follow through on this month.

- Memorize 2 Timothy 2:1-7. Write it out. Say it out loud. Share it with 2 other men in your life this week.

BE FRUITFUL AND MULTIPLY

So God created mankind in his own image,
in the image of God he created them;
male and female he created them.

God blessed them and said to them, **"Be fruitful and multiply and fill the earth and subdue it.** Rule over the fish in the sea and the birds in the sky and over every living creature that moves on the ground."

GENESIS 1:27-28

God is the ultimate Farmer and you are His handiwork.

In the beginning, we see God creating. Working. He worked, then He rested. The pinnacle of His work was the creation of mankind in His image. God then blessed them and gave them the overarching command for humanity. *"Be fruitful and multiply. Fill the earth and subdue it."*

Among many other profound truths in the opening words of the Bible, there are two fundamental realities that are rock-solid essential for MEN: to know who they are and what they are supposed to do with their lives.

IDENTITY and PURPOSE.
Identity and responsibility. Being and doing.

Together, these point to the overarching purpose of man's existence. To know and glorify God. That's no small claim, and it's no small longing in the soul of a man.

Have you ever asked questions like:

Who am I? Why am I here? What am I supposed to do? What's my role and contribution? What's my job?

At various stages and phases of a man's life and journey, these questions may come with varying degrees of intensity.

➡ Perhaps you're a young man looking to his future with all the potential options of paths to choose.

➡ Or maybe you're starting out on a path and still wondering if there's more to life, if you're going to somehow miss out on something even better.

➡ Perhaps you're approaching or entering midlife and wondering if what you're doing now is really what you're going to do for the rest of your life.

➡ Or maybe you've achieved some success, accomplished some things, and built up a retirement but still wonder about the significance of it all. Maybe questions of ultimate impact and legacy are starting to consume your quieter moments and thoughts.

Welcome to the inner questions and longings of what it means to be a man. What a journey. What a life.

The good news is that God has answers for all those questions. He put them there deep in your soul, so that you would look to Him for the answer. He created you. And He calls you.

Genesis 2:15

The Lord God took the man and put him in the Garden of Eden to work it and take care of it.

He holds the key to your identity and your purpose. It's all found in Him. He's not hiding, but you still have to search.

If you have eyes to see and ears to hear, you can find it right here in Genesis chapters 1 and 2. It can put you on the adventure of a lifetime. These truths are the catapult your soul craves—climb on to be launched in the direction of greatest satisfaction and impact.

IDENTITY | The Imago Dei

We were created in the image of God. That's a mind-bending mouthful.

What does that even mean?

The meaning of the '*imago dei*' has been contemplated for centuries. As men, we need to think about it, wrestle with it, reflect on it, and seek to understand it.

It's unique and significant. It's the deepest root for the intrinsic worth, value, and dignity of life. Life is sacred and precious. And human beings are the pinnacle of God's creative work.

To be made in the image of God means we are, in a special way, His representatives. Additionally, we were made embodying something of the attributes and capacity of the Creator. Humans were given faculties of knowledge, imagination, intellect, reason, will, desire, and capacity for relationship with God beyond the rest of the created world.

Who are you? What are you?

The deepest root of your identity as a man is that you were created in the image of God.

You were made *by* God and *for* God.

> ### Three Approaches to Identity
>
> - Eastern thought says you're an illusion. Fulfillment is found by becoming detached from this world. **Become who you need to be by detachment.**
>
> - Secular thought says you're the result of random chance. Therefore, you can randomly determine and declare your own identity. **Become who you need to be by self-declaration.**
>
> - But Christianity gives a third and very different answer. **You are the result of intentional design.**

You did not create yourself, you're not an illusion, and you do not self-determine your identity. You receive it. You become who you were created to be by embracing God's design.

The error of the secular mantra today, which has been repackaged time and again throughout history and inevitably leads to the unraveling of society, is that man can self-determine his core identity.

It is a destructive lie from the pit of Hell. It's being sold and forced on the masses as I write this. Don't buy it.

It's impossible to fully live into the reality of your life calling and purpose as a man, as a farmer (provider and worker), without first embracing by faith this fundamental reality: **You are who and what God says you are.**

PURPOSE | The Creation Mandate

God has not only created you, He has blessed you. He has given you a big job and significant responsibility. He has given you an overarching purpose.

Be fruitful and multiply. Fill the earth and subdue it.

There are two essential parts that were given. Multiply and manage. Populate and cultivate. Family and vocation. That oughta keep you plenty busy.

Get married. Have kids. Protect them. Provide for them. Lead them. Love them. Then launch them to do the same. Be productive. Bless the world. Discover it, unlock its potential, use it, manage it, and cultivate it all carefully as a steward of God's creation for the flourishing of humanity.

Work the land, grow food, build shelter, build buildings, start companies, paint paintings, write books, grow gardens, make things,

create systems, invent products, design modes of transportation and communication, study, teach, explore, train animals, harness energy, organize things, support things. Cause people and communities to thrive. Promote human flourishing.

Humans were to populate the earth and create culture. Take what He has made, take what He has given, and work with it. Mold it, build it, multiply it. Manage it, subdue it, rule over it.

Like a shepherd with a flock. Like a farmer with a field. Like a father with a family.

The Creation Mandate is no small thing and it touches EVERY PART of your life and the purpose for your very existence.

As a man, you were created with incredible purpose—to know God. To live in relationship with God. To work with and for God.

Sin entered the story through our own rebellion and defiance…and royally jacked things up.

But the command remains in effect. And Jesus showed up to save us and restore us to live out that original calling by issuing a new call.

"Follow me."

RESTORED IDENTITY & RENEWED PURPOSE
The Great Commission

After dying on the cross as a substitutionary sacrifice for sinners and rising again from the dead on the third day, He found His disciples and gathered with them on the mountain. Even as some doubted, He said to them, "*All authority in heaven and on earth has been given to me. Therefore go and make disciples of all nations, baptizing them in the name of the Father and the Son and the Holy Spirit, and teaching them to obey everything I have commanded you. And surely I am with you always, to the very end of the age.*"
Matthew 28:18-20

God's purpose for our lives is to know Him and make Him known. To be restored in relationship with the Father through the Son by the Spirit. To glorify Him and serve Him by fulfilling His call on our lives to be fruitful and multiply, to be productive, creative, providers, and multipliers. To make babies and to make disciples. To work a job and make a difference as representatives and ambassadors for Jesus.

Be fruitful and multiply. Fill the earth and subdue it.

Get a Wife. Family. Job. Church.

Dream it, build it, create it, expand it, manage it. Cultivate it.

Identity, purpose, calling, responsibility, contribution, significance, legacy.

It's all right here. In a life that is from and for God. Restored and renewed in Jesus.

FROM A STRONGER MAN

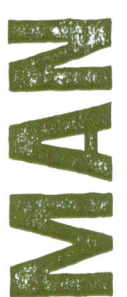

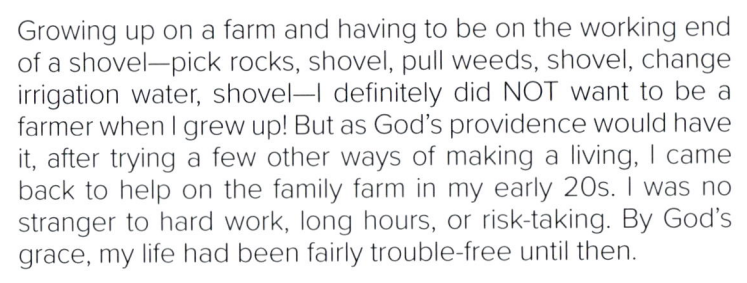

FARMER

Growing up on a farm and having to be on the working end of a shovel—pick rocks, shovel, pull weeds, shovel, change irrigation water, shovel—I definitely did NOT want to be a farmer when I grew up! But as God's providence would have it, after trying a few other ways of making a living, I came back to help on the family farm in my early 20s. I was no stranger to hard work, long hours, or risk-taking. By God's grace, my life had been fairly trouble-free until then.

I got married at age 22 and I'm not blaming my wife, but............ that's when the trouble started. :) In all seriousness, that IS when the trouble started because I was all in, 100% devoted and committed to the farm, and I expected my lovely new bride to support me with that same devotion. However, our relationship steadily started producing "bad fruit" and I pretty much blamed her. I was busy spending most of my time, energy and attention nurturing crops. I thought I was being the "provider" God had called me to be, but my "providing" was misdirected towards things (crops can be idols, too) instead of people. My lovely bride and newborn son were being left in the dust.

Looking back 40 years, I can see God's grace to me by putting in our path a pastor and his wife that ministered to us through their Godly marriage teaching. **My wife and I slowly started to learn some marriage skills and began following Christ in every area of our lives.**

I share this past because I think every man has to battle with that work/life balance, no matter what vocation you are in, and it is not easy to accomplish! But I can now thankfully say, by God's grace, my wife and I have celebrated 40 years of marriage and have been blessed with 3 children and 5 grandchildren, so far. :) Now, 40+ years later, we are still operating a successful farm operation.

As I reflect on my years of farming, I believe God has taught me much about Himself and His purpose for me. And the older I get, the more I've learned to trust him. We have had many crop failures over the years due to hail, high winds, excessive heat, early freezes, late freezes, rain, pests, weeds, disease, and a large dose of my own ignorance and stupidity! So, I preach to myself the truth that God is not only in charge of the weather, but the cause of it! That'll keep you up at night wrestling with your theology! I have relied on the stories in scripture, Jesus' parables, and thoughts from Godly men to sustain me through hard times. I've written Godly wisdom down in my pickup, in my office, in my phone, and in my mind.

Genesis 3:17 *Because of Adam's sin, God cursed the ground so it would produce thorns and thistles.*

Job 38:3-4 *"Brace yourself like a man....Where were you when I laid the earth's foundation? Tell me if you understand."* God then goes on for 4 chapters letting Job know who made the earth and everything in it! Including the rain, hail, ice, wind, lightning, etc.

And when I've laid awake at night totally stressed out over things out of my control, I recite the beginning and end of King Jehoshaphat's prayer from **2 Chronicles 20**, *"Oh Lord...we do not know what to do, but our eyes are on you."*

I remind myself of John Piper's words: "The Bible does not share the modern view that the aim of life is the absence of hardship"

I recite **Luke 12:15** *"...a man's life does not consist in the abundance of his possessions."*

I look at the plaque on my office wall:

Habakkuk 3:17-18 *"Though the fig tree does not bud and there are no grapes on the vines, though the olive crop fails and the fields produce no food, though there are no sheep in the pen and no cattle in the stalls, yet I will rejoice in the Lord, I will be joyful in God my savior."*

I think of Peter's reply to Jesus, when Jesus asked him if he was going to leave too—"Lord, to whom shall we go? You have the words of eternal life"

So I get up in the morning, put on my boots, grab my shovel, get in my pickup, go to work, praise God for who He is and ask Him to help me love my family well.

Galen, 63

REFLECT & DISCUSS

1. What is your biggest takeaway from this chapter?

2. Describe a time in your life where you really thought about, explored, or wrestled with one or more of the "big questions." (Who am I? Why am I here? What am I supposed to do with my life?...). How did you resolve those questions? How often do you revisit those questions?

3. What's the danger of having your identity rooted in something trivial, vulnerable, transient, or self-determined?

4. Why is a sense of purpose and meaning so critical and important? What happens when you lose your sense of purpose?

5. What currently needs your attention in order to be more fruitful, to better care for, to better manage, to cultivate what God has given you? Identify the first 3 steps toward doing that.

6. What are you most proud of to date (in a good way) of something you've produced, built, made, managed, cultivated?

7. What is something in the future you would love to do, build, make, accomplish, contribute, or produce? What's a dream or idea that excites or motivates you?

TAKE ACTION

- Write out a one sentence identity statement anchored in God's work, not your own (in other words, not based on what you do but on what God has done and says about you). *I am a ...*

- Write out a one sentence purpose/calling statement. *I exist to...*

- Review your list of most important relationships from chapter one. Identify 3-4 folks that you will practically bless or encourage this week. What will you do?

WEEK 3

PROVIDE FOR YOUR HOUSEHOLD

Give the people these instructions, so that no one may be open to blame. Anyone who does not **PROVIDE FOR THEIR RELATIVES, AND ESPECIALLY FOR THEIR OWN HOUSEHOLD,** has denied the faith and is worse than an unbeliever.

1 TIMOTHY 5:7-8

The root meaning, or etymology, of the word "provide" comes from the Latin 'providere,' meaning "look ahead, prepare, supply, act with foresight" (from pro "ahead" + videre "to see").

Hence, provision is just that—pro-vision. To supply in advance. To see ahead and act accordingly.

In fact, provision always follows vision. Money, resources, supplies. These only come after there's a vision of somewhere to go and what is needed to get there.

To provide is a responsibility that is at the heart of manhood.

Men are to be providers.

We are to see ahead, to prepare for and supply what our families need. That's our job.

Stronger men act with foresight. Weak men wait around for someone else to bail them out.

Stronger men pull their own wagon. Weak men, and little boys, want to ride in someone else's.

How do you know when you're a man? Well, are you a puller or a rider? That's not the whole answer, but it's an important part of it.

In these verses (1 Timothy 5:7-8), Paul is giving Timothy instructions for how to teach and lead Christians and churches to maturity. Specifically, in the surrounding context, he is addressing the reality of widows in need and how to assess who needs help and who qualifies for assistance from the church.

There are always situations where people are in need of help, and certainly, the Christian life is a generous, merciful, neighbor-helping way of life. But there are times when there are people in proximity to those needs who should be the ones to step up and step in to meet them. Or when the person in need themselves can and should be a part of their own provision.

Elsewhere, Paul wrote, "If a man will not work, he shall not eat." (2 Thessalonians 3:10)

In essence, Paul is saying, we don't just give money to everyone who asks for it. Assess each situation. If people are able to work and provide for themselves in their situation, that's exactly what they should do. If there are friends and family around a widow or a person in need, don't rob them of their responsibility and opportunity to be a part of the solution.

That's part of the dignity of being human. That's what makes a strong family, a strong church, and a strong society. If someone is always pulling you around, you're going to get weaker, not stronger. That's not good for anyone.

Here's the reality: handouts often hurt more than they help.

You want to give a gift to someone? By all means—yes and amen—give!

It is wise, though, not to cultivate an immature and ungodly form of dependence between one in need and one able to offer assistance. Especially in the basic needs of life. We each are called to work to earn the bread we eat.

The temptation of irresponsible, sinful people, apart from the work of the Spirit, good instruction, and good example, is to look for someone to come along and do it for us. Give it to us. Bail us out.

We live in a work-averse, entitled, get-rich-quick-addicted world.

Everyone wants to take the elevator. No one wants to take the stairs.

Not stronger men. Stronger men take the stairs. Stronger men pull the wagon. Stronger men provide for themselves and their families.

Weak men want something for nothing. We are seeing the results of an entitlement mentality and ideology that is raising a generation to think they "deserve" to have things given to them. To have it easy. To get to bypass the stairs of hard work, intentional saving, and frugal spending.

You know what that produces? Spoiled, ungrateful, entitled brats who are a drag on society. There's nothing generous or compassionate or helpful about that.

So dads, how do you keep your kids from becoming spoiled brats? Don't give them everything.

Teach them the value of hard work, personal sacrifice, diligence, patience, planning, saving, budgeting, contentment, responsibility, and the dignity of carrying their own load and paying their own way.

A pastor buddy of mine says it like this, "Men are like trucks. They drive straighter and smoother with a heavy load."

Without the weight of responsibility to provide, men get squirrelly and put their life in the ditch. And usually, they are taking others with them.

Men need to start working at a young age and learn the lessons afforded by menial, low-paying jobs. Minimum wage jobs are there for a reason. They are entry level so that people learn the value of work and the value of a dollar earned. Higher paying jobs require hard work, hustle, ingenuity, and sometimes study and schooling. Providing financially as a man involves taking risk, producing value, and generating income.

If you want to have a family and fulfill your biblical responsibilities of providing for your family, you need to work hard, study hard, pay attention, and choose a career path that gives you the opportunity to earn or create a living wage that can support a family. You need to learn how to keep your costs and expenses low and make wise decisions with your money.

You'll need to live self-controlled. You'll need to defer gratification. Learn to budget. Live below your means. Give, save, invest, and spend wisely.

But it starts with vision. Look ahead, prepare in advance, and act accordingly. That's what farmers have to do. That's what men need to do.

SOME FINAL THOUGHTS:

This doesn't mean your wife can't or shouldn't work outside of the home and help contribute to the income of your household. But it does mean that it's ultimately your responsibility, men, to figure it out and take the lead in cooperation with your wife. If you have kids and she's able to stay home for a season and care for the kids and household needs, that too is a noble thing. Each couple will work these things out in unique ways. There are challenging times, financially, that often require the ingenuity and teamwork of a husband and wife both contributing in ways according to their ability to supply the resources you need or desire.

A man's responsibility to provide for his household extends beyond the material provision. We are called to provide in all spheres: material, financial, spiritual, emotional, and relational. Some of you may be incredible material and financial providers but are failing to provide the emotional and spiritual leadership and support that your wife and family need. That too is your responsibility. You're called to pull the wagon in more ways than one.

Don't lose heart! In Christ, you have a Father in heaven, who has promised to provide for you. Where God guides, God provides. He's given you this role and this responsibility, and He hasn't set you up for failure. He will supply the strength, wisdom, and opportunity you need to step into your role as a provider for your family. Trust Him and seek counsel from those who know Him well to help you walk in the way of a stronger man who is providing for his household.

Look for ways to mentor and encourage others. There are many men among us who didn't have an example of a faithful provider in their dad. There are young men who are in the process of trying to figure out what to do and how to provide. Be available to share your knowledge, wisdom, and experience with others. Be generous with your knowledge and life experience. Be ready to encourage and build up the brothers around you.

FARMER

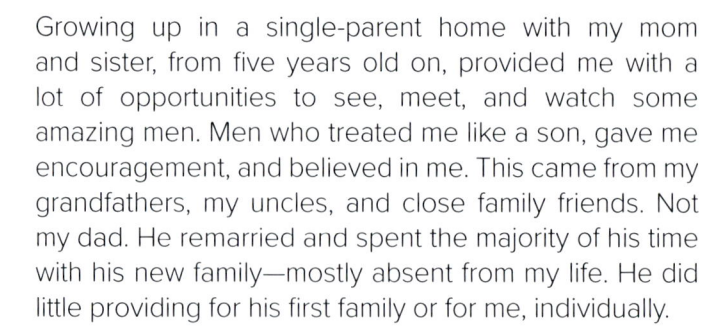

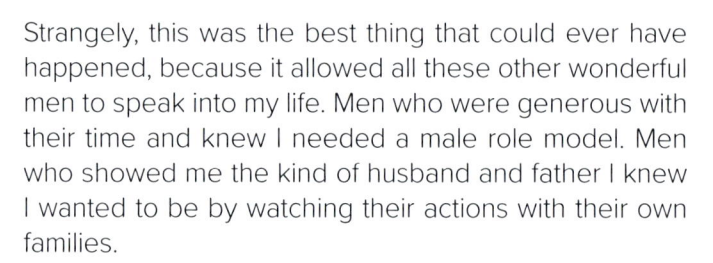

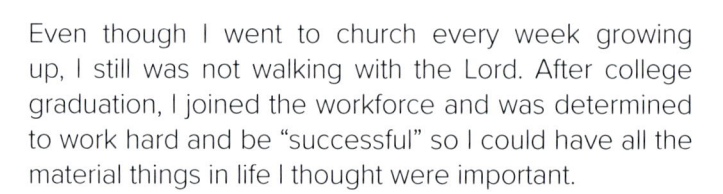

FROM A STRONGER MAN

Growing up in a single-parent home with my mom and sister, from five years old on, provided me with a lot of opportunities to see, meet, and watch some amazing men. Men who treated me like a son, gave me encouragement, and believed in me. This came from my grandfathers, my uncles, and close family friends. Not my dad. He remarried and spent the majority of his time with his new family—mostly absent from my life. He did little providing for his first family or for me, individually.

Strangely, this was the best thing that could ever have happened, because it allowed all these other wonderful men to speak into my life. Men who were generous with their time and knew I needed a male role model. Men who showed me the kind of husband and father I knew I wanted to be by watching their actions with their own families.

Even though I went to church every week growing up, I still was not walking with the Lord. After college graduation, I joined the workforce and was determined to work hard and be "successful" so I could have all the material things in life I thought were important.

That changed in 2000, when I gave myself to the Lord one evening on a boat in Canada. I went from being afraid to die to knowing there is an awesome place for me once the Lord is done with me here on earth. And I realized that the Lord wanted me to share my blessings, instead of accumulating them all for myself. I've learned that there is spiritual and emotional help, not just financial help, to offer others.

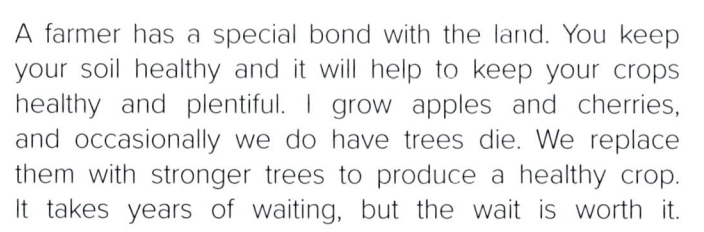

A farmer has a special bond with the land. You keep your soil healthy and it will help to keep your crops healthy and plentiful. I grow apples and cherries, and occasionally we do have trees die. We replace them with stronger trees to produce a healthy crop. It takes years of waiting, but the wait is worth it.

Investing in the lives of my wife, daughters, son-

in-law, grandchildren, and other family and friends is the same concept. It takes years to see the results, but they are worth it. The Lord expects me to take care of those I am responsible for—just like a farmer takes care of his trees—and I try every day to do this better. It is a work in progress, but I daily strive to be more generous with my time and finances with those who I care for. It is what we are called to do.

2 Corinthians 9:6-8

Remember this: whoever sows sparingly will also reap sparingly and whoever sows generously will also reap generously. Each of you should give what you have decided in your heart to give, not reluctantly or under compulsion, for God loves a cheerful giver. And God is able to bless you abundantly, so that in all things at all times, having all that you need, you will abound in every good work.

I thank the Lord every day for my awesome, supporting wife of almost 30 years and my two simply amazing daughters.

Robb, 61

REFLECT & DISCUSS

1. What is your biggest takeaway from this chapter?

2. What are some of the jobs you've had over the years or in your earlier years? What helpful lessons did you learn or character did you develop from those jobs?

3. Why is the entitlement and handout mindset dangerous for men? What does it produce?

4. In what areas would you say you're currently doing a good job as a provider? Where do you need to improve? What would it take to do that?

5. How can you help teach and train the next generation to work hard and provide for their family? How will you ensure that your sons and daughters know the value of hard work and provision?

_____

_____

_____

6. What are some examples of things you see potentially in the future (near or far term) that you need to begin preparing for and taking action now?

_____

_____

_____

7. In what ways do you experience fear or anxiety related to providing for your family? What truth about God or promises from His word do you rely on to help encourage you?

_____

_____

_____

TAKE ACTION

- Make and/or revisit your personal financial budget. Are there any changes that you need to make?

- Revisit your retirement and insurance situation. Are you prepared and preparing to provide for your family in the future?

- If God is leading you to explore or consider a change in your vocation, seek out wise counsel, get unified with your wife if married, and prayerfully take action to move in the direction of God's leading.

- Identify one thing you need to begin preparing for and start taking action this week. Take the first step.

WEEK 4

STRONGER MEN ARE GIVERS NOT TAKERS

Anyone who has been stealing must **STEAL NO LONGER,** but must work, doing something useful with their own hands, that they may have something to share with those in need.

EPHESIANS 4:28

Have you ever stolen something? Be honest.

I have. More than I like to admit. In fact, there was a rebellious time in my life, before I knew Jesus, when I had a habit of stealing. In particular, cigarettes and batteries.

Talk about an arrogant, naive, warped, entitled perspective! It's crazy, I know. But inwardly, in my rebellion, I told myself a man shouldn't have to pay for smokes and he shouldn't have to pay for batteries to run his CD player, because, after all, you shouldn't have to pay to listen to music. Ugh. Gross, I know.

It was also a dirty thrill. The arrogance and rush of "getting away with it." It all fostered the classic sinful attitude of "I'll do what I want and you can't stop me." "Watch this." Pure rebellion. Stealing. Taking. Sin.

It's really a picture into the sinful heart of man. It's the stuff of small, weak men.

Before you get too far down the road of judging me (though I entirely deserve it!), let's consider other kinds of stealing that might have your name on them.

There are lots of ways to steal. Lots of ways we men are "takers."

- When you're late—you're stealing time. (Thanks for teaching me this, Pastor Kent!)

- When you lie about someone—you're stealing their reputation or their good name.

- When you fudge on your taxes—you're stealing from the government. (Even if it seems they are stealing from you first.)

- When you mess around with a girl sexually—you're stealing her purity.

- And if you ever slept with a girl for the first time who wasn't your wife—you stole her virginity, and you stole from her future husband.

- When you fail to tithe and give to the Lord—you're robbing God.

- When you take advantage of someone in a negotiation and you know it's an unfair deal—that's called stealing.

- If you use dishonest weights & measures—that's stealing.

- When you present someone else's idea as your own—you're stealing their intellectual property and credit.

- When you cut in line—you're stealing from those you cut in front of.

- When you take an extra-long break for lunch, working less than you're being paid for—you're stealing from your company.

- When you are regularly late getting home from work—you're stealing from your wife and kids.

- When you break your promises with your family—you're robbing them of a man they can trust.

- When you make yourself the center of attention—you're stealing others' opportunity to contribute or participate.

- Above all, and included in all of the above, when you make life about yourself, seeking selfish glory, living for yourself—you're a taker—stealing glory that belongs to God alone.

Need to revisit your initial answer to my opening question?

The fact of the matter is, whether you can specifically identify with one, all, or none of those examples, apart from Jesus, we are takers.

We all, like sheep, have gone astray.

We've all robbed God and we've all taken from others. The good news of the gospel is that there is hope for thieves like you and me!

One of the ways you can see the power of Jesus in someone's life is when a taker becomes a giver.

FARMER

There is a fundamental shift that takes place when a man begins truly following Jesus.

As Paul is writing to the Ephesians, he knows there are people who are being saved and rescued out of a life of sin. People are being brought in to relationship with Jesus. So Paul is instructing them about the nature of the real Christian life.

Notice the progression.

Ephesians 4:28
"Anyone who has been stealing must steal no longer, but must work, doing something useful with their own hands, that they may have something to share with those in need."

Step One: Stop stealing. Copy that.

Step Two: Instead, work. Got it.

Be an honest, productive person. Do something useful with your own hands. Makes sense. But here's where it gets good.

Step Three: Give!

The gospel doesn't just take us out of reverse and put us into neutral. It doesn't just get us to "stop stealing." It doesn't even leave us at the much better place of "work and do something useful with your own hands."

Any average Joe can do that (on the surface, at least).

The transformation to become a stronger man goes deeper than that.

The gospel doesn't just help you "stop doing" the bad stuff. Oh, it does that alright. But it does so much more!

From stopping, most definitely. To working, absolutely.

And then…"that they may have something to **SHARE with those in need."**

Reverse ➡ Neutral ➡ FORWARD!

The change is total. 180 degrees. And there's so much more to a life going forward (joyfully giving!) than going backward (selfishly taking).

To be a stronger man, you don't just stop going the wrong way. You start going the right way, powered by the gospel. (1st, 2nd, 3rd, 4th, 5th gear!)

Jesus transforms takers into givers.

The gospel leads us out of a life of taking, into honest, productive working, and on into the high ground and high-speed adventurous life of generous giving.

Stronger men no longer steal. They work. And they don't just work to earn and produce honestly. They work, earn, and produce honestly so that they can give generously.

Stronger men are those who have been changed, and are being changed, from takers to givers in every area of life.

What gear are you in?

Where do you need to change from being a taker to being a giver?

Where do you need to start moving forward?

Where might God be calling you to step into Spirit-led generosity?

FROM A STRONGER MAN

My story is a long one—a work in process and the Lord is still shaping and growing me today. My focus is to share that true joy comes from a life of redemption and a life of using our natural, God-given talents to bless others.

Thirteen years ago, the Lord was literally crushing me under the weight of my unrepented sin. I would lay in bed at night unable to sleep, thinking that I was going to die and go to Hell. God had delivered me from years of heavy drug and alcohol addiction and brought me a new life in some ways. It was Jesus who allowed me to get clean and sober. The Lord had spared my life, but I had not understood my purpose for living. **The reason that I was being crushed became very clear to me. I had a type faith but had not valued the blood of Christ, truly repented, and left my years of addiction-based sin at the foot of the cross.**

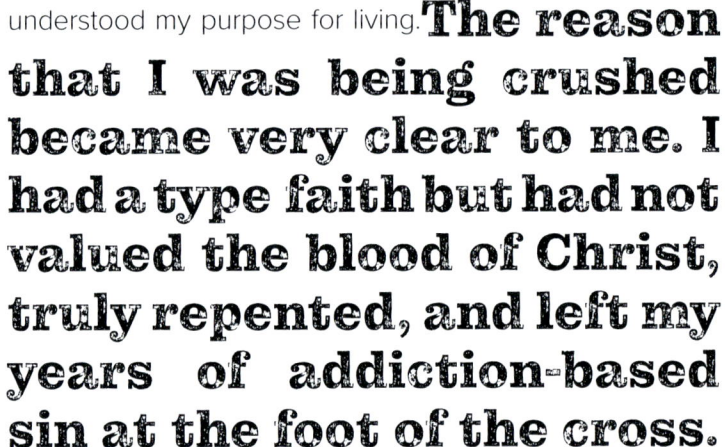

I had not yet understood salvation, only survival. My survival mode and false pride created incredible motivation in me around work and financial production. I was literally hell-bent on catching up after wasting more than half my life mired in grotesque and debilitating addiction. The gains I had made in my life were completely centered around self, materialism, and manly image. I had become Mighty Mike in my own eyes. I still wasn't right with Jesus—trying to serve two masters is impossible. Through fellowship with other godly men, I learned about being really saved, and I repented. I finally felt FREE. I no longer lived in fear of God, guilt, and self-hatred. The Holy Spirit was moving in me and revealing there was more.

Life had gotten so much better, yet there was another process underway. I began to understand the difference between repentance, which was in my misguided case almost solely focused on saving myself, impossible as it was, and the practice of living to glorify God. This was a slower growth period of first working to die to self. I still was a man who had earthly idols, tried to portray an image of worldly success and chasing after things of the material world. My life was still lacking true joy and direction. I began to reflect on my purpose, how God had blessed me, and where I could make an eternal impact on God's Kingdom and HIS people. God must have more for me. If not, why did he save me from myself? I began to think eternally about my life and what my legacy would be. My wife and I had always been generous but never focused on real purpose in our generosity. I knew it felt good to give gifts and had a generous spirit. I began to see that the Lord had given me specific gifts as a unique man made in His image. I was gifted with good business instincts, vision, and a can-do attitude. How could I use my specific God-given gifts to glorify God instead of self or family?

Serving others is one way—serving the bride of Christ is another. That led me to a clear understanding that God had saved me from death to help build HIS Church. I have often been able to counsel and come along others in the struggle of addiction and always feel great rewards through that blessing. However, the greatest joy, and most exhilarating sense of purpose for me, has been in financial gifting and vision-casting for HIS Church. I came to the realization in life that all I had and all that I have built is only because the Lord has allowed it. All the money and all the possessions were His and I was just a shepherd or manager of them. I needed to use them to HIS glory! My entire countenance and reason for living the earthly journey had moved from myself to glorying God with my life. I still sin, repent of sin, and need to be challenged. God's Word, God's Church, and godly men through community are a huge part of my life. I now seek a greater purpose for living in light of eternity, and I have true love and joy as a result. My mantra—Die to Self, Live for Jesus, Glorify God, and Focus Eternally!!

Mike, 60

REFLECT & DISCUSS

1. What is your biggest takeaway from this chapter?

2. What specific, tangible changes has Jesus made in your life? What are some "before & after" examples?

3. What did you most identify with in the list of "ways we steal" in this chapter? Are there any that you would add?

4. Where do you need to change or keep changing from being a taker to being a giver? What needs to stop in your life? Where do you need to start moving forward and what would that look like?

WEEK FOUR

5. Where might God be calling you to step into Spirit-led generosity?

___

___

___

6. Is it hard for you to receive someone else's generosity? Why do you think it can be hard for men to accept or receive someone else's generosity? What is good and what is not good about that?

___

___

___

7. Who has been an example and model of hard work and generosity to you in your life? How have you experienced the generosity of someone else in your life? What was that like?

___

___

___

TAKE ACTION

- Look up and carefully read 2 Corinthians chapters 8-9. What big ideas and takeaways related to generosity and giving do you see in those chapters? What stands out about the Corinthians? How does it relate to Jesus and the gospel? Make a list.

- Is there something that needs to STOP in your life? Share with one or more brother(s) in Christ and invite their prayers, encouragement, and accountability.

- Identify one opportunity/need to be generous toward and bless someone tangibly this week. What was the result of you taking that action?

WEEK 5

WORK WITH ALL YOUR HEART

Whatever you do, **WORK AT IT WITH ALL YOUR HEART,** as working for the Lord, not for men, since you know that you will receive an inheritance from the Lord as a reward. It is the Lord Christ you are serving.

COLOSSIANS 3:23-24

Therefore, my dear brothers and sisters, stand firm. Let nothing move you. Always **GIVE YOURSELVES FULLY TO THE WORK OF THE LORD,** because you know that your labor in the Lord is not in vain.

1 CORINTHIANS 15:58

Stronger men give their best effort.

How you work matters. Is there anything worse than half-hearted effort?

"Meh."

"Eh."

"Whatever."

"Who cares?"

"It doesn't matter."

"Good enough."

"Oh well, it's not that big a deal."

THAT IS NOT THE ATTITUDE OF STRONGER MEN. That's not the way of a faithful farmer. Let's break down work a little.

Here are four important aspects of work.

1 WHAT you do. As men, we are to engage in honest, honorable, and helpful work. There are countless jobs and kinds of work that fit into those categories. Blue collar, white collar, and everything in between. Bank robbing isn't one of them. Selling drugs doesn't make the list either. If you don't have a clear and compelling sense of a particular calling, that's okay. Find something you enjoy and are capable of doing well and go for it. You can even try multiple things. There really are an incredible number of options to make a living. And when your work is ultimately for the Lord, all of it is Kingdom work. It will give you opportunities to bring Jesus to the marketplace and display His Kingdom through your productivity, in your relationships and by your results. **Stronger men do good work.**

2 WHY you do it. There's a lot of talk in the world about "finding your why." It's not uncommon to hear un-compelling answers. Worldly motivation is empty and vain. It's easy to end up chasing mere stuff. But it is true that you need a real and significant "why." If you don't know why you are doing what you do, the motivation won't last. Drudgery or doldrums will set in. Or you'll succeed in something pointless. There are great, compelling reasons to work. For starters, so you can eat. For men, it's pretty simple. Men are made to work. So you work to be responsible. To pay your bills. To provide for your family. To bless others. For the satisfaction of a job well done. To benefit others. To contribute to society. To provide jobs for others. To do good in the world. To stay active and healthy. And ultimately, chief of all, to glorify the Lord. **Stronger men know the ultimate why and remind themselves often.**

3 WHO it's for. This is connected to your why, but it's good to drill down and be clear. A lot of men have poured out blood, sweat, and tears all in an effort to try and win the approval of their boss (or their dad). And part of that can be healthy. It's good to want to honor and carry on the legacy of your dad or the family business. To do a good job for your boss or employer. To work for your family. All of those are good and right in their proper place. But ultimately, seeking to please men will fail you. It becomes a form of bondage—a weight that crushes men or leads to compromised principles and convictions in an effort to appease someone. Our work can also become purely selfish. We can make it all about me, myself, and I. **Stronger men ultimately work as unto the Lord. God is the one we are working for in the end.**

4 HOW you work. That's where these verses in Ephesians and First Corinthians come in. How are men to work? The answer is, "with all of your heart." Because our work is good, meaningful, and unto the Lord, we give our best effort. "Always give yourselves fully to the work of the Lord." Whatever work you find or the Lord gives you to do, give it your all. Give your best effort. Do the best you can do. **Stronger men live and work as men who are working for the Lord, for His glory, for the good of others, with all our hearts.** It's a glorious, powerful, compelling, contagious, freeing, and rewarding way to live.

Ecclesiastes 9:10

Whatever your hand finds to do, do it with all your might.

1 Corinthians 10:31

And whether you eat or drink or whatever you do, do it all for the glory of Christ.

Picture two men washing dishes...

One of them is frustrated, eye-rolling, irritated, impatient. Doing a sloppy job, missing a spot here, breaking a dish there, all the while thinking of all the other places he could be and all the other things he could be doing. Grumbling under his breath that the house work isn't already done and subtly resenting his wife and kids who had the audacity to ask him to help. Don't they know that he's been working hard all day? Don't they appreciate the way he provides? He bought the groceries after all. He shouldn't have to make the food or do the dishes. His irritation grows and he's moments away from barking out a snide comment that will set the tone for the

FARMER

whole house for the rest of the night—likely ending in an argument and the exasperation of those around him. That's one way to do dishes. A weaker (and foolish) man's way.

The other man is whistling, smiling, focused, carefully cleaning each dish and handling each dish with care. Steadily accomplishing the work. He's reminding himself of how grateful he is to be in this home the Lord has provided, to have the unspeakable blessing of a wife and children he gets to eat with and laugh with and serve and watch grow in the grace of God. He sees the leftover bits of food, plunging his hands in the soaking pot to grab the next plate. Wasn't that a new recipe his wife and daughter tried tonight? He's grateful that his daughter is eager to learn and try as she prepares to be a wife herself some day. He silently says a quick prayer for that special young man, wherever he is. He then looks down and sees the dried spaghetti sauce. He persistently scrubs away every red stain, the sponge and soap unveil the clean white dish beneath it. In an instant—in his mind's eye—he sees the power of Jesus' forgiveness that has cleansed his own soul. He remembers the promises of the Lord removing each stain and washing him clean. He looks over his shoulder to see his wife is finally off her feet. They catch a glance and smile. The night ends with peaceful conversation, a hug from each child, a grateful "thanks for helping with the dishes" met with, "thank YOU for dinner."

Does that seem sappy or silly to you? Pious or unrealistic? I promise you, that's another way to do dishes. A stronger man's way.

WEEK FIVE

Of course, you can also delegate the dishes to your kids and sit by your wife on the couch and talk about the day. That works too. But I'm guessing you get the point.

How you work makes a big difference. In seen and unseen ways. The attitude and effort. The motivation and satisfaction.

The perspective of a stronger man is that it is a privilege and an honor to serve the Lord and to work with all our heart, whatever we're doing, as unto Him.

One of my favorite songs that powerfully illustrates this point is the Christmas song "The Little Drummer Boy."

When you take out all the "pa rum pum pum pum" drum sounds (which sound cooler than they read), you're left with these lyrics:

Come they told me,
A new born King to see,
Our finest gifts we bring,
To lay before the King,

So to honor Him,
When we come.

Baby Jesus,
I am a poor boy too,
I have no gift to bring,
That's fit to give the King,

57

*Shall I play for you,
On my drum?*

*Mary nodded,
The ox and lamb kept time,
I played my drum for Him,
I played my best for Him.*

*Then He smiled at me,
Me and my drum.*

Stronger men play their best for Him!

I'll take a church full of Drummer Boys all day long. Men who humbly give their best, day in and day out, playing their heart out for King Jesus.

Colossians 3:23-24

Whatever you do, work at it with all your heart, as working for the Lord, not for men, since you know that you will receive an inheritance from the Lord as a reward. It is the Lord Christ you are serving.

"If I could tell the world one thing about what being a farmer is like, it would be that a passionate heart can carry a weary back through an 80 hour work week."

— Luke Woodson Kneuss

FROM A STRONGER MAN

My wife and I started growing cherries in 1985. I had bought a small house and it sat on a couple of acres with a small cherry orchard on it. Later on, after I figured out I liked farming, we bought some bare ground down in Mattawa and over a period of years cleared the ground and planted a much larger orchard. Overall, I loved growing cherries. I especially loved eating them! I also loved the fact that having an orchard provided a place where my sons and countless other teens and young men and women learned to work and work hard. And we were able to bless countless workers, businesses, and our church along the way.

One of the things I did early on in my farming career was to seek out and listen to and learn from other men who were in the business and were successful growers. What I found was that across the board these men's focus was on growing and, ultimately, harvesting dessert quality fruit. To them it was more than a way to make a living, it was something they thought about, talked about, studied, and poured their lives into. **These men were all in, everything on the table, committed farmers. Listening to them talk and watching them work inspired me to do the same.**

It ended up that the work was hard and there were plenty of long days, longer nights, we were cold, wet, hot, sweaty, dirty, bone-tired, and exhausted many, many times. Tacos at the taco stand became our regular diet. There were plenty of frosty nights, trees to be pruned, bugs to be sprayed, diseases to battle, grass to be mowed, and all of the other work that goes along with farming. But at the end of the season when the harvest came in and the fruit was in the bin and washed with water there was nothing so beautiful and satisfying.

Over the years, the more I learn about how trees grow and produce fruit, the more I stand in awe of the plan that God has put in motion. He created the air, the water, the soil, the sun, the trees, bees, and hundreds of other things that all worked in unison to produce fruit. As farmers, He has called us into that process and given us not just a part, but a big part in the plan. And working within that plan we are able be part of something that produces a beautiful harvest.

In 2 Timothy, Paul draws on the image of the hard working farmer because, men, there is another plan that God has set in motion. Another plan that He created and orchestrated and is calling us to be a part of. Our part is not a small part either but a very important part. This is a plan that also leads to a harvest, but not a harvest that is perishable like a cherry, here today and gone tomorrow, but a harvest set for eternity. A harvest of sons and daughter, friends, family and absolute strangers. A harvest that, when brought in and washed with the blood of Christ, is not just beautiful but absolutely glorious. So the questions I ask myself and you are: are you farming, are you all in, everything on the table, committed and pouring your lives into it? Are we working hard and putting in long days and longer nights? Are you hot, dirty, sweaty, bone-tired, grabbing a taco, and jumping back into the field? Because, men, the harvest is plentiful, workers are few, and time is short. So, men, get in the field, do some work, scatter seeds, and start grabbing some low-hanging fruit.

Shawn, 62

REFLECT & DISCUSS

1. What is your biggest takeaway from this chapter?

2. When are you tempted to coast? To not give your best or do your best?

3. Describe the difference and reward of giving your best and "working with all your heart?" What impact does a good attitude and great effort make? Be specific.

4. Who has been a personal example to you of someone who always gave themselves fully to the work of the Lord? What else was true of that person that you could use more of in your life?

WEEK FIVE

5. Is there a situation in your life currently where you are being challenged to do your best and do it as unto the Lord, where you might otherwise be tempted to slack or "mail it in?"

_____

_____

_____

6. **HUSBANDS/FATHERS** What does it look like right now for you to give your best in your marriage as a husband? To your kids as a father? Where do you need to "step it up?"

_____

_____

_____

7. **YOUNG MEN** What would it look like for you to apply these verses to your current season of life? How would it impact your daily routine?

_____

_____

_____

TAKE ACTION

- Look for examples this week, both positively and negatively, of great effort and poor effort, of great attitudes and bad attitudes. What did you notice?

- Memorize Colossians 3:23 and 1 Corinthians 15:58.

- Identify a task or project at home that would bless your wife (or someone important in your life) this week. Go for it. Give it your best. What did you do and how did it go?

WEEK 6

WARNING TO IDLE SLUGGARDS

I went past the field of a sluggard,
past the vineyard of someone who has
no sense; thorns had come up everywhere,
the ground was covered with weeds,
and the stone wall was in ruins.

I APPLIED MY HEART TO WHAT I OBSERVED AND LEARNED A LESSON

from what I saw:
A little sleep, a little slumber,
a little folding of the hands to rest—
and poverty will come on you like a thief
and scarcity like an armed man.

PROVERBS 24:30-34

The Bible has a lot to say about laziness.

Laziness is directly related to poverty and insecurity. Conversely, hard work is directly tied to prosperity and security.

Many have made the case that there's no better way to learn how to work hard than to grow up on a farm. It used to be the only option there was! The industrialization and technological advancement of the modern age has come with some incredible advantages to be sure, and yet, simultaneously, it has introduced some major hurdles and setbacks for men.

Work used to be sun up to sun down. However, as innovation and progress have made life easier on a thousand levels, they've created a whole new experience for humanity: leisure.

We are an entertainment culture. We sit and stare at screens. We sit and watch others pretend and play games. We travel more than any other generation of humans and build garages for our toys and hobbies. We have information and entertainment overload.

All this cultural transformation and advancement is the product of incredible hard work and ingenuity. It's the fruit of the creation mandate unfolding as humans build and create—it's truly impressive.

"But with great power comes great responsibility." I heard that in a movie I watched once. Of a guy who has super powers after getting bit by a spider. I was probably eating popcorn and licorice when I heard it.

This much is true—the need for responsibility in every area of life is as great as ever.

In recent years, through the shared experience that was the Covid insanity, we've seen what happens when good times (freedom and prosperity) make weak men who have forgotten the source and value of those good times. Weak men then make for hard times.

This is actually good news, because hard times make strong men.

In his 2016 post-apocalyptic novel "Those Who Remain," Michael Hopf considers the idea that weaker and stronger generations are cyclically replacing each other throughout history.

The quote from that book that has gone viral is as follows: **"Hard times create strong men. Strong men create good times. Good times create weak men. And, weak men create hard times."**

I don't know anything else about Michael Hopf or his book, but that much he got right. It's been a time of weak men. It's now time for strong men.

As my friend, Pastor Josh McPherson has said many times, "We've been lulled to sleep under the warm blanket of freedom."

"A little sleep, a little slumber, a little folding of the hands to rest—and poverty will come on you like a thief and scarcity like an armed man."

This is true on an individual and collective level.

What is our response? What will we do? What will we teach our sons and daughters and pass on to the next generation?

Up and at 'em, boys!

Let's be clear—there's more than one kind of laziness. The metaphor and imagery of Proverbs 24 applies to *every kind of laziness.* There are lazy workers, sure. There are also lazy thinkers. Lazy husbands and lazy fathers. Lazy Christians and lazy churches. And the results are just as damaging everywhere laziness takes root.

Let's be men who work hard in every way; word, thought, deed, and relationships. Physically, spiritually, financially, intellectually, and relationally.

I picked that particular passage in Proverbs 24 (verses 30-34) because it had the word "sluggard." What a great word. A clear picture of a terrible life.

Notice in the Proverb, a sluggard has no sense.

Have you noticed that common sense is—well—not exactly altogether common these days? We can't even stay clear on the differences between boys and girls.

Thorns and weeds cover the ground of a sluggard's farm.

The walls are in ruins. He's open to attack and pests and the field is in no condition to yield a harvest. He's in real danger of not making it through a hard winter.

How did he get here?

Laziness. Idleness. One extra day off at a time. A little sleep. A little slumber. A little folding of the hands to rest.

But just a little. And a little more. And a little more. There's always a trajectory.

It's the way almost all sin works in our lives as men. "It's just a little bit. It won't hurt. It's not that big a deal. No one will even notice. Just relax! Take it easy. That can wait."

The net result is poverty coming on "like a thief" and scarcity "like an armed man."

For years I've said it this way: The suddenly is often made up of the subtly.

How did I get here?? Men wonder aloud as their marriage is in shambles. Their kids are off the rails. Their finances are a mess. Their health is out of control. They're bound in addiction.

You got here one little step at a time. One little decision at a time. One moment for correction neglected at a time. One little break at a time. One little slip up at a time. One little sin at a time. One little outburst at a time. One little, flesh-driven verbal jab at a time. One little broken promise at a time. One little put down at a time. One little bite at a time.

"How did this happen?!" "Hey, we're out of bread?!" "The pantry is empty—what are we going to do?!" "My marriage is crumbling?!" "My kids are walking away from God?!"

You can hear the shock and surprise in the panicked voice of the sluggard.

"Help!"

But to those with wisdom, to those who observe and consider the outcome of people's lives, it's not always a surprise.

"Did you hear? So-and-so left their wife. So-and-so lost their job. So-and-so is struggling again." (Not as a form of gossip, but as concern for prayer and a brotherly or pastoral desire to help).

I don't mean to sound callous. It's not that I don't have compassion. Let's help the weak. Let's support and encourage each other, yes and amen. But remember: an ounce of prevention is better than a pound of cure.

You may fancy yourself a hard worker, and you probably are, at least in one area of your life. But take a broader look. Step back and ask, where am I in danger of being lazy? Where am I letting thorns and weeds grow in my soul? In my relationship with God? In my marriage? With my children?

Where is the wall torn down? Where am I vulnerable to pests? Where am I slacking off? Where are little compromises starting to add up?

Friend, don't let the subtleties become the sudden-lies in your life.

Subtle neglect becomes sudden defeat.

Don't be idle. It brings all kinds of destruction, disruption, and disrepute to the reputation of men and of Christ.

Here are two more passages on the dangers of idleness to consider as we bring this chapter to a close:

1 Thessalonians 5:12-15

Now we ask you, brothers, to acknowledge those who work hard among you, who care for you in the Lord and who admonish you. Hold them in the highest regard in love because of their work. Live in peace with each other. And we urge you, brothers and sisters, warn those who are idle and disruptive, encourage the disheartened, help the weak, be patient with everyone. Make sure that nobody pays back wrong for wrong, but always strive to do what is good for each other and for everyone else.

FARMER

2 Thessalonians 3:6-13

In the name of the Lord Jesus Christ, we command you, brothers, to keep away from every believer who is idle and disruptive and does not live according to the teaching you received from us. For you yourselves know how you ought to follow our example. We were not idle when we were with you, nor did we eat anyone's food without paying for it. On the contrary, we worked night and day, laboring and toiling so that we would not be a burden to any of you. We did this, not because we do not have the right to such help, but in order to offer ourselves as a model for you to imitate. For even when we were with you, we gave you this rule: "The one who is unwilling to work shall not eat." We hear that some among you are idle and disruptive. They are not busy; they are busybodies. Such people we command and urge in the Lord Jesus Christ to settle down and earn the food they eat. And as for you, brothers and sisters, never tire of doing what is good.

Up and at 'em boys. Let's set an example worthy of diligent farmers.

LET'S BE STRONGER MEN.

"And on the 8th day, God looked down on his
planned paradise and said, "I need a caretaker."
So God made a farmer.

God said, "I need somebody willing to get up before dawn, milk cows,
work all day in the fields, milk cows again, eat supper and then go to town
and stay past midnight at a meeting of the school board."
So God made a farmer.

"I need somebody with arms strong enough to rustle a calf and yet gentle
enough to deliver his own grandchild. Somebody to call hogs, tame
cantankerous machinery, come home hungry, have to wait lunch until his
wife's done feeding visiting ladies and tell the ladies to be sure and come
back real soon -- and mean it."
So God made a farmer.

God said, "I need somebody willing to sit up all night with a newborn colt.
And watch it die. Then dry his eyes and say, 'Maybe next year.' I need
somebody who can shape an ax handle from a persimmon sprout, shoe a
horse with a hunk of car tire, who can make harness out of haywire, feed
sacks and shoe scraps. And who, planting time and harvest season, will
finish his forty-hour week by Tuesday noon, then, pain'n from 'tractor back,'
put in another seventy-two hours."
So God made a farmer.

God had to have somebody willing to ride the ruts at double speed to get
the hay in ahead of the rain clouds and yet stop
in mid-field and race to help when he sees the
first smoke from a neighbor's place.
So God made a farmer.

God said, "I need somebody strong enough to clear trees and heave
bails, yet gentle enough to tame lambs and wean pigs and tend the pink-
combed pullets, who will stop his mower for an hour to splint the broken
leg of a meadow lark. It had to be somebody who'd plow deep and
straight and not cut corners. Somebody to seed, weed, feed, breed and
rake and disc and plow and plant and tie the fleece and strain the milk and
replenish the self-feeder and finish a hard week's work with a five-mile
drive to church.

"Somebody who'd bale a family together with the soft strong bonds of
sharing, who would laugh and then sigh, and then reply, with smiling eyes,
when his son says he wants to spend his life 'doing what dad does.'"
So God made a farmer."

— Paul Harvey

FROM A STRONGER MAN

I'm proud to be a farmer. I believe it's the grandest of occupations. Not because of profits or lifestyle but because it affords you the opportunity to work in partnership with God and His creation every day.

Modern farming has been commercialized, and while it's still a very noble way to make a living, what I want to talk about is farming in its purest form. I want to talk about the dirt, the plants, the water, the sunshine, and how we mold them into life-giving food for all of us. But most importantly, I want to talk about how God uses all of it and the experiences farming provides to reveal Himself to us.

God gave humans dominion over the earth and all its plants and animals in Genesis, giving rise to the world's first occupation. In doing so, He invited all men into a partnership of sorts between His Kingdom and all who dwell within it. A partnership where you can do maybe 10-15% of the work and reap 100% of the bounty, and even though that sounds like the deal of the century, it doesn't end there. In accepting this occupation, you learn the gift of HARD WORK. Yes, you heard that right—the gift of sleepless nights, worrying about cold and hot weather, digging, plowing, fixing, weeding, mowing, chopping, spraying, feeding, harvesting, and on and on. *But wait,* you say, *I thought you said it was a gift? That sounds really hard!* Dang right it's hard, and thank God for it. Thank God He knows our hearts and what we yearn for.

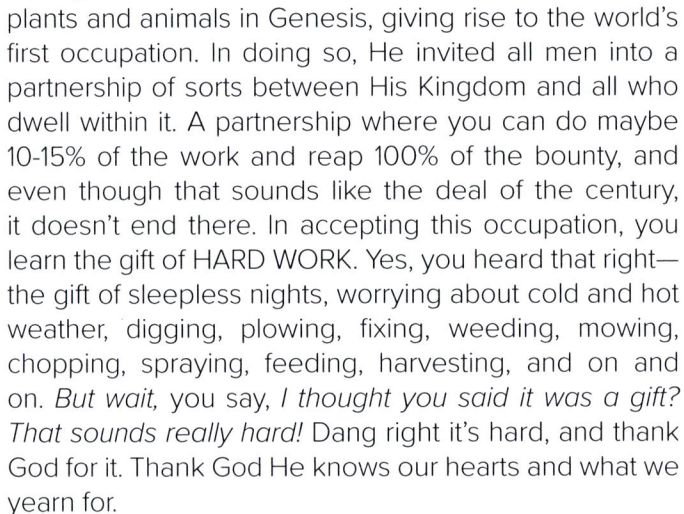

As a boy, my dad would drag us off to the orchards when school was out in the summer. We would ride motorcycles, shoot BB guns, run through the sprinklers, and eat tree-ripe cherries and peaches. Later, as I grew, he taught me to drive tractors, prune, mow, spray, fix broken sprinklers, set bees, start wind machines, and light smudge pots in the dead of night. The burden of the work caused me to grow wary of the farm. I couldn't wait to do anything but toil in the orchard.

As a young man, I went away to college and began to realize I missed the farm and the work. I missed the time with my dad, I missed the struggle of the work, I missed feeling the gratification of a job well done. I missed seeing those delicious cherries, pears, and apples stacked high in our loading pad ready to travel to the warehouse. I missed the smell of fresh air. The chill of a full moon, the frosty mornings. The smell of apple trees in bloom. I missed the first explosion of flavor that comes once a year in a fresh cherry or a tree-ripe apple.

Looking back on my life, having raised my family on my own farm, I have gained perspective and gratefulness. You might remember, I referenced doing "10%-15% of the work" and getting to reap a 100% bounty. I'm not trying to belittle the roll we play as humans. It is extremely important. We have all seen fields left untended. They all look the same—full of weeds, dead plants, and decaying infrastructure. This is where my perspective comes in. You see, I now recognize that farmers play a vital role in the raising of the crop. If we didn't tend the crop, it would be far less bountiful. But I believe this is where the partnership with God comes into play. You see, while we toil to "raise" the crop, we would be powerless without the fertile soils which supply the nutrition, the moisture, the counterbalance to keep the plant upright. The sunlight which triggers and provides for the complex chemical reaction within the plant (the photosynthesis) which turns sunlight into stored energy. The water, which is the perfect delivery vehicle for nutrients from the soil into the roots and out to the leaves and fruit. The water also carries the converted sunlight energy to the roots to feed them. The plant itself, which knows exactly when to grow, when to bloom, when to ripen, and when to rest. That's what I mean when I say humans do 10-15% but God does the heavy lifting and we get 100% of the benefit.

But there is more... **There are days when the work takes all your strength and you can barely stand, early mornings when your bed feels so good and you have a hard day ahead but you get up anyway, and times**

FARMER

FROM A STRONGER MAN

when you're drying your cherries after a summer rain storm to keep them from cracking and praying they won't split. You have a front row seat to the awesome power of the nature He created for us. Those are the necessary days! The days that forge your soul into steel. Those are the days that galvanize you as a man. The days that teach you to lead, teach you to endure, teach you to overcome adversity. That is why it's a gift! Our God and Father has given us a profession that gives us value, confidence, toughness, and tenderness and He lets us do it alongside of Him! Working a farm is a symphony between man's struggles and God's miracles...a truly special partnership between Creator and caretaker.

Tim, 50

Blessed is the one who does not walk in step with the wicked or stand in the way that sinners take or sit in the company of mockers,
but whose delight is in the law of the Lord, and who meditates on his law day and night. That person is like a tree planted by streams of water, which yields its fruit in season and whose leaf does not wither— whatever they do prospers.

Not so the wicked! They are like chaff that the wind blows away. Therefore the wicked will not stand in the judgment, nor sinners in the assembly of the righteous.

For the Lord watches over the way of the righteous, but the way of the wicked leads to destruction.

— Psalm 1

FARMER

REFLECT & DISCUSS

1. What is your biggest takeaway from this chapter?

2. Where are you in danger of allowing subtle forms of idleness and sloth to cause problems in the future?

3. When are you tempted to be lazy?

4. What's the hardest thing about your current job/work?

5. How would you describe or define the difference between unhealthy laziness and healthy rest?

WEEK SIX

6. "Subtle neglect becomes sudden defeat." How have you seen this transpire in your life or in situations close to you?

_____

_____

_____

7. **HUSBANDS/FATHERS** What does it look like for you to be lazy in your marriage and in your parenting and how can you guard against it?

_____

_____

_____

8. **YOUNG MEN** When are you tempted to be lazy? Where is laziness showing up in your life currently and how can you fight against it?

_____

_____

_____

TAKE ACTION

- Look for examples this week, both positively and negatively, of hard work and laziness, of diligence and neglect. What did you notice?

- Make note of if and when you're tempted to be lazy this week. Make and have a plan to be corrective and be productive instead.

- What's one thing you've "let slide" that you could give attention and energy to this week? Where could you begin to "repair the wall" or "pull the weeds" in your home or work?

- **Bonus: Husbands, ask your wife, "where/when do you see me being lazy or in danger of being lazy?" Listen without being defensive, thank her for her honest feedback, and take whatever corrective action necessary.

WEEK 7

BREAK UP YOUR UNPLOWED GROUND

Sow righteousness for yourselves,
reap the fruit of unfailing love, and
BREAK UP YOUR UNPLOWED GROUND;
for it is time to seek the Lord,
until he comes and showers
his righteousness on you.

HOSEA 10:12

Stronger men embrace the pain of the plow. They know the way of repentance.

There are two fields. Two kinds of lives.

The barren and the fruitful.

The dead and the living.

The boring and the bursting.

You will be one or the other.

Without hunger, you won't work for the harvest. If you don't care, you won't farm. Your fruit will be small and bitter, if it grows at all.

There's no shortcut. There's no easy path. The way is narrow. The ground is hard. The field is fallow. Only a heart of repentance knows the rain of God.

Do you want to be a stronger man? Do you want to know God? Do you want to be a blessing to your family? Do you want to be a part of the Kingdom of God advancing in your lifetime?

Do you desire a fruitful life marked by the presence, power, and peace of Jesus? Do you long for personal, spiritual revival and renewal? Do you want to know God, personally, in a life-changing, life-defining, legacy-altering way?

Friend, if there's even a spark of a fire that says "yes" to any of those questions, there is one way forward. **It's time to seek the Lord.**

It starts with the plow; it starts with repentance.

It's time to break up your unplowed ground. It's time to pray for rain to soak the land. Sow the seed; take in the Word of God. Then pray for the sun—the light and warmth of God's grace—which exalts a humble heart. Then pray for more rain showers. Grow, grow, grow! Then pray for the roots to go down deep, for a faith that perseveres. And pray for the fruit to grow big and tall. Then wait on the Lord, stand in awe, and be amazed.

Is this not the process of farming? Is this not the way of the fruitful field?

Without the pain of the plow, the seed sits on the surface, gets plucked away by the birds, or is trampled underfoot. The hard-packed soil isn't open to receive water and the seed has no room to open, nowhere to send down roots, and no way to take in life-giving nutrients.

You must embrace the pain of the plow. You must embrace the heart-breaking work of the Spirit of God leading you to repentance as you seek the Lord for His reviving work in your own soul.

The unplowed field produces little fruit. So, too, the unplowed life. But as A.W. Tozer said, "miracles follow the plow." Miracles follow repentance.

God is after our hearts. Yet it's so easy to get stuck in a rut, going through the motions, or never even caring to begin with. As it was in the days of Isaiah, so too in the days of Jesus: *"You honor me with your lips but your hearts are far from me."*

Farming and agriculture provide numerous powerful metaphors throughout the Bible of the true nature of Christianity and the realities of spiritual life.

From the pen of Old Testament prophets to the parables of Jesus, we are shown image after image and story after story of fields, soil, seed, water, rocks, roots, gardens, plants, trees, vineyards, vines, branches, fruit, and harvest.

You, my friend, are a ball of dirt. You are a field. Your life will reap a harvest of one kind or another. For your life to bear the kind of fruit that

will last, to yield the kind of harvest that pleases the Lord, your soul needs plowing.

Where is the Lord working in your life? Where does He need to work next?

Open the gate, let the plow in.

Is there unconfessed sin in your life? In your past? Is there stubborn resistance and pride in an area that you've marked off-limits—"NO TRESPASSING"—for the Lord to do His work?

Where is there a pocket of callousness, a section of stagnation, a rock of cynicism, a root of regret? Where is there the shame of failure, the embarrassment of secrets, the guilt of sin?

Have you ever cried alone in the presence of God?

God is not playing games with you. He doesn't play games with us.

He stands at the door and knocks. He stands at the gate and waits. He wants your soul to thrive.

For that to happen, there must first be a breaking.

Have you been broken before the Lord? Not because of the hardness of your circumstances but because your eyes have been opened to the hardness of your heart and the holiness of God?

Lord! Forgive me for wandering so far away and waiting so long to return! Forgive me for keeping you at arm's length for fear of the pain! Forgive me for caring more about meaningless things and not taking to heart the eternal destiny of my friends, my family, and my own soul!

Forgive me for running after the applause of man, choosing the forbidden fruit, and drinking the mixed wine of seduction.

Let the pain of the plow come in. Break up my unplowed ground. Soften my hard heart. Tear away my self-defenses. Root out my rebellion. Lead me to repentance. Draw me to my knees. Silence my excuses. Shatter my fake dreams. Show me the cross of Jesus Christ.

Rain down righteousness upon me. Capture my attention. Open Your Word to me and fill the dry cracks of my soul with the soothing water of Your Word.

Plant the seed of truth deep in the fresh soil of my heart. Remind me that the violence of the plow is evidence of your unfailing love.

Rescue me from fruitlessness. Save me from barrenness.

Pour your rescuing love upon my dry soul.

Hosea is an incredible book in the Bible. It's a gripping story of how God calls a prophet to marry a prostitute—a living metaphor of His unfailing love for unfaithful Israel. It's a call to repentance. To return to the Lord that we might experience His mercy and love anew.

There's a demonstrable pattern and cycle throughout the Bible and throughout history of people turning away from God, falling on destitute times, crying out to God in desperation and repentance, being met by God's powerful mercy and restoration, only to get complacent again—and so the pattern continues. Fruitful. Barren. Fruitful. Barren. Drawing near. Falling away. Repenting. Retreating. Seeking. Forsaking. Obeying. Forgetting.

Let's be fruitful men with fruitful fields.

Stronger men embrace the pain of the plow.

Hear from a stronger man, A.W. Tozer (1897-1963, American pastor and author):

> The fallow field is smug, contented, protected from the shock of the plow and the agitation of the harrow...But it is paying a terrible price for its tranquility: Never does it see the miracle of growth; never does it feel the motions of mounting life nor see the wonders of bursting seed nor the beauty of ripening grain. Fruit it can never know because it is afraid of the plow and the harrow.

> In direct opposite to this, the cultivated field has yielded itself to the adventure of living. The protecting fence has opened to admit the plow, and the plow has come as plows always come, practical, cruel, business-like and in a hurry. Peace has been shattered by the shouting farmer and the rattle of machinery. The field has felt the travail of change; it has been upset, turned over, bruised and broken, but its rewards come hard upon its labors. The seed shoots up into the daylight its miracle of life, curious, exploring the new world above it. All over the field the hand of God is at work in the age-old and ever renewed service of creation. New things are born, to grow, mature, and consummate the grand prophecy latent in the seed when it entered the ground. Nature's wonders follow the plow.

FARMER

FROM A STRONGER MAN

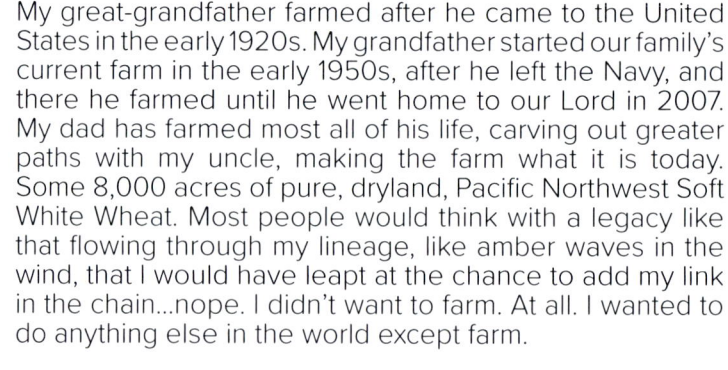

My great-grandfather farmed after he came to the United States in the early 1920s. My grandfather started our family's current farm in the early 1950s, after he left the Navy, and there he farmed until he went home to our Lord in 2007. My dad has farmed most all of his life, carving out greater paths with my uncle, making the farm what it is today. Some 8,000 acres of pure, dryland, Pacific Northwest Soft White Wheat. Most people would think with a legacy like that flowing through my lineage, like amber waves in the wind, that I would have leapt at the chance to add my link in the chain…nope. I didn't want to farm. At all. I wanted to do anything else in the world except farm.

The tedious cycles of plowing, planting, harvesting, praying for rain and maybe enough money to do it again the next year never appealed to me. This was, of course, until I left my home on the Waterville Plateau and realized that there was an ache in my heart—a knowledge that I was not doing what I ought to be doing. "I am a man of the field. I am a farmer." I have now been on the farm full-time for nine years, and if I had not come home to farm, I wouldn't have the greatest love of my life to share in all the ways God has blessed me, namely my darling bride of three years, Alyssa, for whom I am utterly thankful to know and love.

Now, in those nine years of farming, one thing has become absolutely, undeniably obvious: I do not have to plant weeds to make them grow—they are self-evident. If there is dirt, there will be weeds. Russian thistle, mustard, milkweed, kocha, marestail, and morning glory, just to name a few. Not only are they a perennial parasite, but they grow in conditions in which most produce-bearing crops will dwindle. No rain? Excessive heat? No problem. They will grow. And where the weeds are growing, your wheat will not be. So how do we mitigate this problem before the weeds have grown and begun to suck up the vital nutrients we need for seeding? Field maintenance. We work our ground with diligence, making sure we foster a seedbed that will be hospitable for our wheat. We supplement the ground with the nutrients it needs to produce a successful harvest. And we pray for the rain to meet the needs of a growing stand of wheat, knowing that the Lord provides all of our needs.

These practices are as crucial to the stronger man's life as they are on my wheat farm. What weeds do you see growing in your life that need to be plowed over and killed? What kinds of valuable nutrients are they taking from your heart and soul? How are you supplementing

WEEK SEVEN

the faith in your heart? Are you even? Are you being lazy and looking at the weeds in your field saying, "Meh, they aren't that bad yet." Something my dad has drilled into me over the years is that a few things happen to farmers who don't take care of what they have.

The weeds they let grow will spread throughout the field. The owner of that field will take it away from you. The farmer who comes after you will spend years fighting the mess you didn't. And curse you for it!

Apply that in your own life. What sin is flourishing that you won't deal with? What do you have to lose that God has entrusted to you, a man? And what will you pass on to those who come behind you, namely your sons, that they will have to wage war against for days and years to come? Being a good farmer isn't just about doing my best job today but about doing my best for tomorrow and those that will be there in it.

Take heart from our God, the Master Farmer. "Sow for yourselves righteousness; reap steadfast love; break up your fallow ground, for it is the time to seek the LORD, that He may come and rain righteousness upon you." (Hosea 10:12)

We are promised in Hebrews 11:6 that "Whoever would draw near to God must believe that He exists and that He rewards those that seek Him." This is the time to seek God, and we know what work needs to be done in our hearts and minds. **Plow the fallow earth of your heart, sow into it the seeds of righteousness that is reading God's Word and submitting to His will, reap the harvest of His goodness, and bless those in your life by it.** And then, when the chaff has settled and the grain is in the bins, it's time to bring that tractor out to start plowing again, brother. As we say on our farm, dig deep.

Max, 30

REFLECT & DISCUSS

1. What is your biggest takeaway from this chapter?

2. How would you honestly rate your current level of desire for a closer relationship with God? From 1-10 with 1 being dull/low and 10 being desperate/high. Where is it currently? Where would you like it to be? How do you feel about your answer?

3. Have you ever been "broken" before the Lord? What was that like? Have you had an experience of tearful, desperate repentance? If so, what led to that moment and how would you describe it to someone?

4. Are you aware of any "unplowed ground" in your heart/life currently? Is there a subject/issue that is "touchy" or difficult for you to talk about? What's keeping you from opening up about it?

WEEK SEVEN

5. What is your current practice of Bible reading and prayer? When, where, and how often are you spending time reading the Bible, praying, and listening to God? What would you like it to be? What obstacles or hurdles get in your way?

_____

_____

_____

6. How can we fight against apathy, complacency, and stubbornness in our relationship with God? In other priority relationships (wife, children, family, church)?

_____

_____

_____

7. What encouraged you the most in this chapter? What challenged you the most?

_____

_____

_____

TAKE ACTION

- What is one action step that you can identify and take as a result of this chapter, reflection, and/or discussion?

- Read the entire book of Hosea this week in one sitting (it's 14 chapters—you can read it in 20-30min). What stands out to you? What do you think is the central message/theme?

- In a journal or notebook, or even on a Notes app on your phone, write out a personal prayer this week expressing your desire for God to work in your life, including any needed confession and repentance.

WEEK 8
ALL MEN REAP WHAT THEY SOW

Do not be deceived: **God cannot be mocked.** **A MAN REAPS WHAT HE SOWS.** Whoever sows to please their flesh, from the flesh will reap destruction; whoever sows to please the Spirit, from the Spirit will reap eternal life. Let us not become weary in doing good, for at the proper time we will reap a harvest if we do not give up.

GALATIANS 6:7-9

"*Sow a thought and you reap an action; sow an act and you reap a habit; sow a habit and you reap a character; sow a character and you reap a destiny.*" Ralph Waldo Emerson

All men reap what they sow. This is a universal spiritual principle.

Notice in Galatians 6 the danger of being deceived. Deception is one of the enemy's greatest weapons. He is a deceiver. He slithered into the first garden like a snake to deceive a man and his wife about a tree and fruit.

"Did God *really* say that? That won't *really* happen."

The deception in the first garden started with calling into question the integrity of God. Will God really do what He says? Did God really mean what He said?

And what did that deception lead to? Action. And that action resulted in devastating consequences.

That same pattern continues to be played out in every one of our lives.

We see here in Galatians 6 the clear truth that God cannot be mocked. You can't "trick God" and get away with sowing one thing but reap something different. God doesn't say one thing but mean something else.

That's not how it works.

You don't plant corn and grow tomatoes.

"You reap what you sow."

This is actually a very simple, straightforward, elementary principle with nearly limitless applications.

What are you currently sowing?

Well, what are you currently reaping?

What do you want to reap in the future?

The nature of sin is deceptive. Satan always wants us to think that we are the exception, that the consequences won't come.

In the larger context of Galatians, Paul is wanting these Christians to know the power of the true gospel and the freedom of life in the

Spirit that it produces. No other gospel leads to that freedom. No other gospel produces that fruit.

There is a clear contrast between the fruit of the Spirit and the acts of the sinful nature.

FRUIT OF THE SPIRIT VS SINFUL NATURE

Fruit of the Spirit	Sinful Nature
Love	Sexual Immorality
Joy	Impurity and Debauchery
Peace	Idolatry and Witchcraft
Patience	Hatred
Kindness	Discord
Goodness	Jealousy
Faithfulness	Fits of Rage
Gentleness	Selfish Ambition
Self-control	Dissensions
	Factions and Envy
	Drunkenness
	Orgies, and the like

They are in total conflict with each other. They both have opposing desires. They both speak. They say, "Feed me." The one you feed will get stronger.

Stronger men learn to recognize and prefer what the Spirit desires, that which pleases the Spirit, instead of the cheap and easy path of pleasing the flesh.

It's cheap and easy in the moment, but costly and hard in the long run. Such is the deceiving nature of sin.

Sin will take you further than you wanted to go, cost you more than you wanted to pay, and keep you longer than you wanted to stay.

Getting caught in sin is like getting caught in a briar patch. You don't get out easy, and you often need help from others.

This is why just a few verses before this (Galatians 6:1) Paul addressed how to handle a brother caught in sin and says to "*restore him gently.*"

Sin has its own price and takes its own pound of flesh. The last thing a brother needs is you to smear his face in it, beat him up over it, or drag him back through it.

But be careful when pulling a brother out of the briar patch; you have to make sure you don't get entangled yourself.

The sinful nature is always close at hand.

As brothers in the battle together—in the field together—we help each other *get out* of the briar patch and *stay out* of the briar patch. But our helping each other has its limits.

At the end of the day, each one of us needs to test our own actions (Galatians 6:4). "*For each one should carry his own load.*" (Gal. 6:5)

What are you sowing? Which voice are you listening to? What choices are you making?

We are each responsible for what we plant and what we harvest—for the path we take and where we end up.

There is a healthy tension in Paul's vision and description of Christian accountability and Christian responsibility. We are called to help each other and, simultaneously, we are reminded that we are 100% responsible for ourselves.

If you're in a group of men as you read or discuss this, think about the benefits of pursuing stronger manhood together. We encourage each other. We support each other. We pray for each other. We spur one another on. We identify with each other many times and in many ways.

What is often talked about in many men's ministries, as the "holy grail" of men's groups, is "accountability."

Let me be clear: I'm for accountability. However, I also want to be clear that accountability has significant limits.

Sometimes we think accountability means you are responsible for helping me stop sinning or helping me do what I should. *Hey brother, hold me accountable.* Which might mean simply—ask me about it. Which is great.

But at the end of the day, a large majority of Christian men who have fallen in sin, even Christian pastors and leaders who have had moral failings, a large percentage of them were in "accountable" relationships or groups. So what happened?

Simple—they were deceived. So they lied. They were in the appearance of accountability, but inwardly they weren't actually responding to the Holy Spirit. And when you are deceived, it's only natural for you to deceive others.

Deceived men deceive men.

When you believe the lie of the enemy that you can keep sowing to the flesh and not reap destruction, you end up lying to others and, eventually, you reap destruction.

What we need more than accountability to each other is accountability to the Holy Spirit. We need personal responsibility before God Himself. And that's what Paul is teaching. Help restore a brother, help carry each other's load. But watch out. Be sure you keep carrying your own load. Don't just be accountable. Be responsible.

Don't be deceived. God is not mocked. You'll reap what you sow—not what you tell others but what you actually do. God sees. God knows.

It's either flesh or Spirit.

There's a brother reading this who is tired. Discouraged. Defeated. Worn out. Farming is tiring. Sowing is hard work. And sometimes it doesn't look like anything is growing or is ever going to grow.

Brother, don't grow weary in doing good! Don't stop fighting! Don't stop planting! Don't stop confessing and repenting.

For at the proper time, we will reap a harvest if we don't give up.

Keep sowing to the Spirit. Keep farming. Keep going. Keep growing. God sees. One day, it'll grow. Soon, it will break the surface. Soon, it will bear fruit. One day, the fruitx will ripen.

One of the greatest ways you can help your brothers is by simply setting a fruitful example. God will display the fruit. As if to say, "How do you like them apples?"

Stay the course. Don't be deceived. God is not mocked.

Listen to the Spirit. Do what pleases Him. You'll never regret it.

> But by the grace of God I am what I am, and his grace toward me was not in vain. On the contrary, I worked harder than any of them, though it was not I, but the grace of God that is with me.
>
> — 1 Corinthians 15:10

FROM A STRONGER MAN

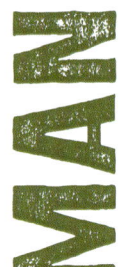

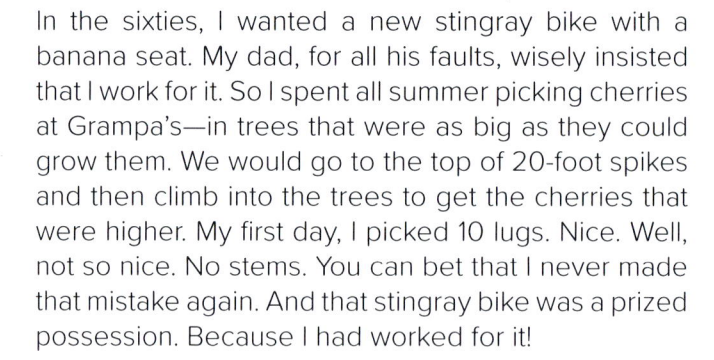

In the sixties, I wanted a new stingray bike with a banana seat. My dad, for all his faults, wisely insisted that I work for it. So I spent all summer picking cherries at Grampa's—in trees that were as big as they could grow them. We would go to the top of 20-foot spikes and then climb into the trees to get the cherries that were higher. My first day, I picked 10 lugs. Nice. Well, not so nice. No stems. You can bet that I never made that mistake again. And that stingray bike was a prized possession. Because I had worked for it!

All of my young life was spent in the orchards and hills of the upper Wenatchee valley. We owned several orchards, as did my grandparents. Unfortunately, after an ugly divorce, my father sold them all.

My mother took us to the coast when I was 11. Not good. Luckily, I ended up in sports and the coaches and the comradery kept me off the streets. When I came of age, my mother insisted that I go to college. My father had dropped out of high school to go to WW2. He came home a hero and finished high school, but he carried angry scars. So my mother insisted on college for me. Let's just say that WSU was a waste of my parents' money and of my brain cells.

Then I was off to California with all my possessions in my little car and not a soul to see. I ended up working construction (piecework) and boy did we work. Then came speed (amphetamines). A lot of my buddies used in order to work harder and faster. I thank God for the memory of that stingray, because I wasn't about to give my hard-earned money to the pusher man.

California wasn't all bad. As a matter of fact, it was miraculous. I met a beautiful lady and I met my Lord and Savior. In that order. I had memories of my grandparents—their wonderful marriage and their godly example—so I said, "there's the girl and there's the church."

After almost 40 years, it has been awesome. The work has been hard, at times, but oh-so-worth-it.

When we moved back "home" to the valley, I brought with me a wife and four kids and a desire to buy an orchard. People in-the-know were quick to tell me that I was crazy. Eventually, we bought a nearly abandoned orchard. Then I knew what they were talking about.

It is work and lots of it, sunup to sundown. But it's good work, and God will bring the harvest.

My dad and I have had many personal struggles, but God's grace is new every morning. My earthly father was not able to, but my Heavenly Father tells me daily how much He loves me.

Writing this, I realize that I need my eyes checked because of these blurry spells I keep experiencing reliving the Lord's faithfulness.

We now have 10+ grandchildren all being raised in the faith. We continue to live on the farm, and it's good to watch the 6th generation experience the good life.

Jim, 67

REFLECT & DISCUSS

1. What is your biggest takeaway from this chapter?

2. How do you experience the conflict between the flesh and the Spirit? When have you been aware of that war/conflict during the last week? Today?

3. What are some practical ways you can daily/weekly sow to the Spirit? What are some common ways you're tempted to sow to the flesh?

4. What are your thoughts about the differences and strengths/limitations between brotherly accountability and personal responsibility? Why is it important to make that distinction?

WEEK EIGHT

5. **HUSBANDS/FATHERS** How can you lead your wife and family to sow to the Spirit and not the flesh in the home? What are some ways you can apply this right now? What kind of leadership/farming will that require from you?

6. **YOUNG MEN** What does sowing to the Spirit look like for you at this stage of your life, and why is it so important? How is the enemy trying to deceive you and others in your generation about the nature of sin?

7. When are you tempted to be discouraged? How do you fight off discouragement? What promise is given in Galatians 6:9 and how can you leverage that to your advantage?

TAKE ACTION

- Read the book of Galatians this week in one sitting (takes about 15 minutes). What insights jump out at you?

- Pray with and for your wife and kids out loud every day this week. What was the fruit of that action/effort?

- Identify one habit that you need to start and/or one habit that you need to stop. What would happen if you maintained/stopped that habit for the rest of this month? Year?

WEEK 9

STRONGER MEN AND THE FOUR SOILS

A farmer went out to sow his seed. As he was scattering the seed, **some fell along the path**, and the birds came and ate it up. **Some fell on rocky places**, where it did not have much soil. It sprang up quickly, because the soil was shallow. But when the sun came up, the plants were scorched, and they withered because they had no root. **Other seed fell among thorns**, which grew up and choked the plants. **Still other seed fell on good soil**, where it produced a crop—a hundred, sixty or thirty times what was sown. **He who has ears, let him hear.**

MATTHEW 13:3-9

Be sure to refresh yourself with the parable of the sower (Matthew 13:3-9) on the previous page. Jesus went on to explain the parable:

Matthew 13:18-23

"Listen then to what the parable of the sower means: When anyone hears the message about the kingdom and does not understand it, the evil one comes and snatches away what was sown in their heart. This is the seed sown along the path. The seed falling on rocky ground refers to someone who hears the word and at once receives it with joy. But since they have no root, they last only a short time. When trouble or persecution comes because of the word, they quickly fall away. The seed falling among the thorns refers to someone who hears the word, but the worries of this life and the deceitfulness of wealth choke the word, making it unfruitful. But the seed falling on good soil refers to someone who hears the word and understands it. This is the one who produces a crop, yielding a hundred, sixty or thirty times what was sown."

"He who has ears, let him hear."

On a personal note—those are meaningful words to me. Ears actually play a big part of my life story.

When I was born, my ears stuck out. Way out. I was missing a piece of cartilage that holds most people's ears back against their head. As I grew up, they continued to stick out. And as we know, kids aren't always the nicest to one another. So, yeah, I got picked on and called names. I'm not looking for sympathy, but it is what it is. "Hey, Dumbo." A flick here. A flick there. "Did you fly to school today?"

You can imagine the fun that was had at my expense. I was insecure as it was and that certainly didn't help.

But I had a sharp mind and a quick tongue. So by the time I was 7 or 8 years old, I convinced my parents to have a procedure done that would insert the missing cartilage and hold my ears back. I had the surgery in the summer between 1st and 2nd grade. And get this: I had to wear a head cast. Hadn't I suffered enough? It's okay to laugh. At least it was summer and I wasn't in school with that thing. But man it was hot and itchy.

I grew up going to church and there were some missionary friends of my parents who were home that summer. This guy loved Jesus. Gave his life to tell others about Jesus.

He prayed for me and wrote on my head cast: "He who has ears, let him hear."

It was funny. It was also prophetic. I believe he sincerely prayed for me when he wrote it. He prayed for a little boy with a cast around his physical head and ears to one day spiritually hear the voice of Jesus. And eleven years later, God answered that prayer.

That's why that verse means a lot to me now. I have heard Jesus time and again over the years, and there's not a thing in this world you could offer me that I would want in place of that. You can have this whole world, just give me Jesus.

Physical ears are not the point. Spiritual ears are the ones that count. Hearing and understanding the voice of Jesus and following Him, even if no one else is—even when it's hard, even when you're picked on and ridiculed and name called, even when the world looks so much more enticing—that's what counts.

On the Parable of the Sower

Jesus was a master teacher. The parable of the sower is one of His most famous parables. In many ways it's the parable of parables, and it's all about farming.

The secrets of the Kingdom of God are hidden in parables. They are the secrets of being a stronger man.

Don't check out. Don't breeze past this chapter. Listen to me carefully. Listen to Jesus carefully.

It may seem simplistic. Almost elementary. This is a parable we teach to children. But don't think it's beneath you—Jesus taught it to grown men.

And many of them still didn't get it. If we think this is too simple—might I suggest that we are the shallow ones?

I've spent over twenty-four years in pastoral ministry, and I've watched many teenagers and many full-grown men and women exude the characteristics of all four of these soil types in living color. Living parables before my eyes. Some understand, some don't. Some remain, some don't.

He who has ears, let him hear—it's what separates the men from the boys, you could say.

As I reflect on my experiences and observation over the years, it does four profound things: it scares me to death, breaks my heart, causes me to marvel and give thanks, and leads me to prayers of repentance and protection.

Except by the grace of God, I'd be snatched away, dried up, or choked out. And so would you. May it never be, Lord. I don't want that for me, and I don't want that for you.

Where will *you* be in 5 years? 10 years? At the end of your life?

What's going to make the difference? Have you thought about what it might cost you?

Let's break this down a little more, one character and one soil at a time.

THE FARMER

Jesus is the Farmer. He is the Messiah who comes to reveal, proclaim, and usher in the Kingdom of God. He is the great Preacher. The true and final Prophet. The King of the Kingdom. He is Immanuel—God With Us. He is God incarnate, God in flesh. The one who saves. The one who heals. He sees and knows the heart. He spoke and He still speaks. He still sows the seed. The Farmer is diligent, persistent, and generous in His sowing.

THE SEED

The seed is specifically described as "the message about the kingdom," the message of the gospel (good news) of God's Kingdom that has come to set captives free and restore sinful man to God. Some understand it, some don't. It is sown in and on hearts as people hear the message. The seed is abundant. There's plenty of it. It is widely scattered, liberally distributed. It is sown everywhere possible. The Farmer has a rich supply of seed, and He wants it scattered over every inch of His field.

THE PATH

The path represents those who do not understand. They don't get it. They don't want it. They don't accept it. They don't connect the dots. The masses walk along the path. The path is packed down, hard, impenetrable. The seed sits on top—it doesn't sink in. It just lands on the surface. This is your neighbor, your brother, your co-worker, your friend. Wide is the path and many are on it.

THE BIRDS

The birds are demonic spirits. Satan doesn't want people to hear, consider, or understand the Word of God. The evil one comes to snatch the seed away. Birds are threats in the realm of farming. Stinking birds! Demons are real and they love to make people fall asleep in Church. They love to help you forget what you heard. They love it when the preacher sounds like Charlie Brown's teacher in your ears. Anything to get you to move on—keep walking, keep moving—nothing to see here, nothing worth hearing or paying attention to. Write it off in your mind and heart and keep moving. The birds want you to hang on to all the shallow reasons to ignore and reject Jesus. The so-called intellectual reasons. The philosophical. The emotional. As long as you don't slow down and really seek answers. The birds (demons) don't want that. They want to carry every last seed away.

THE ROCKS

The rocky soil represents people who hear the message and quickly receive it, but the soil is shallow. In this environment, a plant quickly springs up but it has no root. As soon as the heat of the sun comes up (trouble and persecution)—"because of the Word"—they quickly wither and fall away. They don't last. There are a lot of men who used to be in church, who used to claim to know, love, and follow Jesus. But now they are nowhere to be found. The price was too high. The cost was too great. The trouble for them wasn't worth it; they didn't have a root that could go down deep enough to sustain them through the heat. Roots are really, really important. Hard times will come—specifically and precisely because you follow Jesus. This reality is increasing in our day and the field is being narrowed. The true crop is being exposed and revealed—only those with roots will remain. Do you have the conviction that will stand the mockery and the attack? When it gets hot, will you wilt?

I've seen many men get excited about Jesus. I've seen men weep and appear to repent and receive Jesus. I've seen them get baptized and sit on the front row in church for weeks. But then something happens. Where'd they go? We see them less. When we do see them, that initial joy is gone. Things have gotten hard. Following Jesus isn't all kicks and giggles. Not everyone else in their life was as excited as they were. Their girlfriend didn't like it. The old friends thought it was a little overboard. *You gonna be all churchy now?* The insults came. The rejection followed. The pain of the separation from the old life and the new trouble that comes is too much. They ask themselves, is it worth it? They end up saying "no."

THE THORNS

In a similar way, the seed sown among the thorns doesn't remain and doesn't bear fruit. It gets choked out by the thorns. The thorns are *"the worries of this life and the deceitfulness of wealth."* The plant sprouts and grows, and—for a time—looks to be doing great. It's right there in the midst of the field. But this time, when things get hard, or when other shiny objects come along, the fear, temptations, and doubts rise. Is Jesus enough? Why can't I have the world too? They fail to wholly trust Jesus and instead grasp for the security, comfort, and pleasures this world offers. They believe the lie that Jesus isn't enough. Their heart, when tested, would rather secure for themselves the things of this world, so they sacrifice their relationship with Jesus and they go along with the crowd.

These people used to sit next to you in church; they used to come to your house to grow in the faith. But they've drifted away. They're not there anymore. There were other options that came along that started to sound like more fun. They went back to the life of the weekend warrior. Back to keeping up with the Joneses: sporting events, cars, boats, motorbikes, trips, adventures, workouts, races. Fine dining. New clothes. Along with other world-chasing friends. And the social media posts to go with it. It's all too common. It's pretty sad to watch. Soon, following Jesus and prioritizing the Kingdom of God is a thing of the past. It was a short-lived chapter or season in their life. They are now clearly chasing a different harvest. They are no longer producing the fruit Jesus intended. They've moved on. They're finding the applause, comfort, and security they crave in the things of this world. Don't be fooled: they may look happy today, but they won't be in the end.

THE GOOD SOIL

And then there's the good soil. The good soil represents people who hear the Word and understand it. They produce a crop—30, 60, 100-fold. What started as a small seed has turned into a harvest of obedience, perseverance, and a changed and changing life. That seed has multiplied into the lives of others. Jesus is precious to them above all else. Living for Him is their passion. The power of a seed in good soil is incredible. There are fields, trees, and orchards inside a single seed. A plant with roots, not surrounded by thorns, will weather the storm, the drought, and the heat. It remains. Year-after-year. And it keeps yielding fruit and multiplying crops of its kind. It's awesome to see. I've also had a front row seat watching this process unfold in hundreds and thousands of lives.

Stronger men hear the Word, understand it, remain, and produce a crop.

So, what's the condition of your soil? What danger lurks closest?

He who has ears, let him hear.

FROM A STRONGER MAN

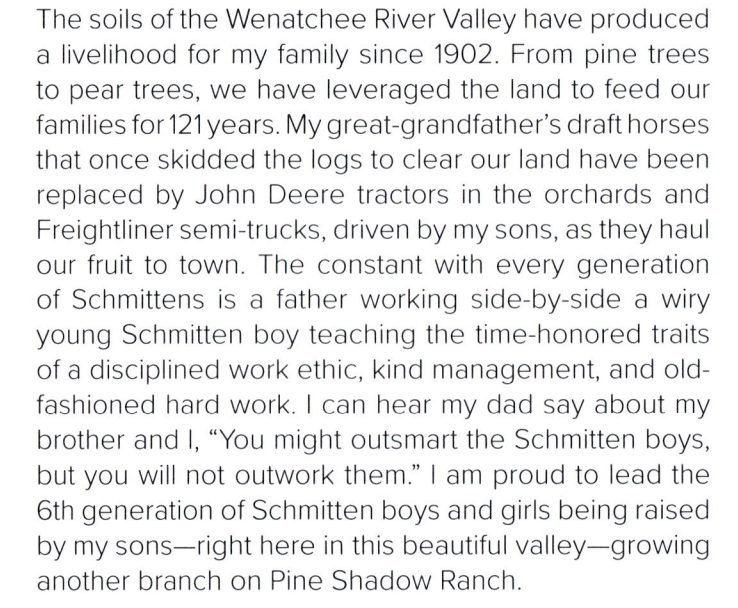

The soils of the Wenatchee River Valley have produced a livelihood for my family since 1902. From pine trees to pear trees, we have leveraged the land to feed our families for 121 years. My great-grandfather's draft horses that once skidded the logs to clear our land have been replaced by John Deere tractors in the orchards and Freightliner semi-trucks, driven by my sons, as they haul our fruit to town. The constant with every generation of Schmittens is a father working side-by-side a wiry young Schmitten boy teaching the time-honored traits of a disciplined work ethic, kind management, and old-fashioned hard work. I can hear my dad say about my brother and I, "You might outsmart the Schmitten boys, but you will not outwork them." I am proud to lead the 6th generation of Schmitten boys and girls being raised by my sons—right here in this beautiful valley—growing another branch on Pine Shadow Ranch.

My wife Trish and I have raised our 4 boys, helped raise a few nephews and nieces, and have enjoyed sharing our family with many other kids needing a loving home. The "home place" on Pine Flats in Dryden has seen every shenanigan a teenage boy can think of.

"The Devil is in the details."

These first paragraphs, while true, would make a better trailer for a show on the Hallmark channel than the true details of my life as a privileged, hardworking, hard-living young man.

While I grew up with the values of the church from my mother and had a Bible by my bed most nights of my life, I have strayed often from walking with my Lord. I patterned my life more through the ballads of Hank Williams Jr. and Lynard Skynyrd than a faithful follower of Jesus: "Whiskey Bent and Hell Bound" would be a fitting song title.

Lots of parties, DUI's, college rodeo lifestyle, and an odd pride that went with being bounced from every bar in a college town.

Regardless of lifestyle, I pursued agriculture straight out of college with a degree in Horticulture, Tree Fruit Production, from WSU in 1985.

I worked as an Ag Consultant in Wenatchee Fruit Warehouses so I could get a down payment to buy into my family's pear orchard in Dryden, WA in 1987. Finally, I was a "farmer." I was growing food from the soil to the table.

Life continued to provide opportunities for me and my family.

Expansion of our farms was followed by a partnership in a fruit packing warehouse. My little farming venture was now becoming a vertically-integrated ag business.

"If you get half of your wishes, you'll double your trouble."

By the time I was in my mid-thirties, I had surpassed my dreams and secured most of my goals. **I was full of myself and far from walking with the Lord. It was time for the lessons to begin—one humbling event after another.**

Fruit prices took a dive, retailers demanded more services, and technology investment in fruit packing was required. The search for investment money coincided with partners filing bankruptcy. Divorce struck my marriage with plenty of fault on my shoulders. The fragile house of cards which was built on energy, greed, and young arrogance crumbled. It was time to go back to the basics: back to the farm, a good job, and eventually putting God and my family back into my life. I always wanted a big family, and I was soon blessed by meeting a woman of parallel values. The great reset began.

FARMER

Without the strength and unbending faith of my wife, Trish, I would never have been able to be the father and family leader I needed to be. The Lord blessed me with her presence in my chaos, and she has helped me grow into who I am today. I am not perfect but improving. Together, we searched for a church where we and our youngest boys could lean into the teachings of the Bible. We found a community that could help us align our lifestyle with Christian values.

Farming as a lifestyle has been the root of good things in my life. The family comradery that is built after we pulled together to plant a new orchard. The fulfilling feeling of finishing a two-month long harvest. The last load of fruit being hauled to the warehouse for the year. And, as always, the memories of the harvest parties in October.

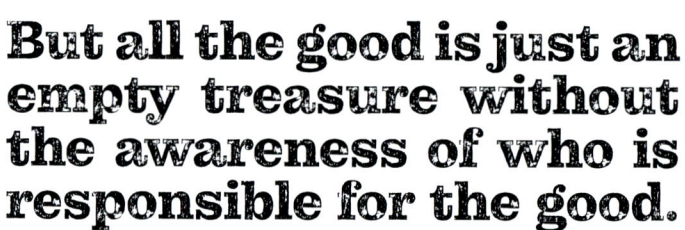

But all the good is just an empty treasure without the awareness of who is responsible for the good.

Who provided the sun and the soils and the air and the water? Who walked with you through the trouble? Who smoothed the arrogance and lifted you when your own stupidity wrestled you to the ground?

Farming comes with the challenges of nature, wind, hail, heat, drought. Society then stacks on the additional headwinds of labor, government regulations, and taxes.

Now add the fact that the farmer is human—his life will create its own tragedy, strife, depression, and sleeplessness. So how many opportunities for failure does a farmer have before that first pear gets sold at market? They seem too numerous to count.

"I believe in the faith of a farmer, tailgate prayers and a Bible on the dash."

As an ag consultant, fruit warehouse manager, farmer, and a striving Christian, I see the parallels Jesus brings to us in life and on the farm. The best farmers I know observe and embrace both success and failure. They try to duplicate success and avoid the failure. As one seeks who they are as a parent or a leader we must see the target clearly. Look for the models to emulate and, without judgement, avoid following those who are not proper role models.

Then surround yourself with successful people and the model is right in front of you.

In his letter to the Corinthians, Paul points out that you may have planted the seed but God gives the growth. You are God's field—God's building. Through our own actions, we can do God's work and He will give us growth.

Ray, 60

REFLECT & DISCUSS

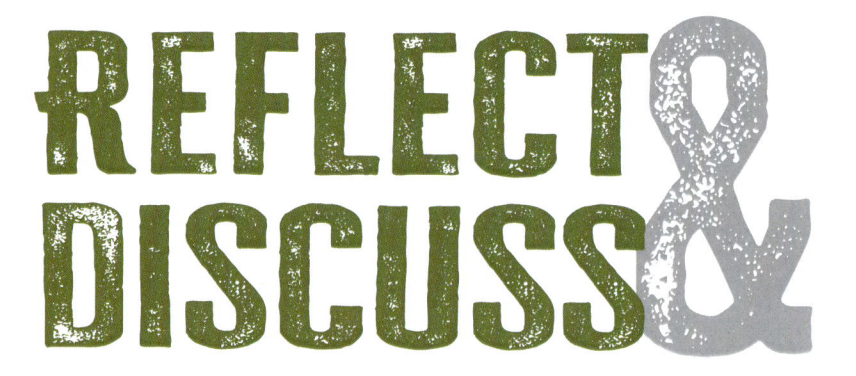

1. What is your biggest takeaway from this chapter?

2. When did you first hear about Jesus? Take a moment and think of when, where, who, and how you first heard about Jesus. How have your thoughts/views about Jesus changed since then?

3. Has there been a time in your life where you understood the gospel message and personally received Christ? How would you describe what that was like?

4. Where is God leading you to sow gospel seed today? Who is God leading you to pray for and talk to about Jesus?

5. Where do you hope to be spiritually in your relationship with God in a year? Two years? Five years? What's your plan to keep growing and bearing fruit?

_____

_____

_____

6. Which of the conditions of the soil (path, rocks, thorns) are you most tempted or threatened by (lack of understanding, persecution, worries, wealth)?

_____

_____

_____

7. How can you guard against your faith being plucked away, drying up, or being choked out? How can you cultivate good soil in your life?

_____

_____

_____

TAKE ACTION

- Where possible, reach out to the person/people who first told you about Jesus this week and thank them! A text, a note, a call. Or identify someone who has encouraged you in your faith and reach out to thank them.

- Using question #5—initiate a conversation with your wife, family, or a close friend this week.

- Write a note in a journal (or on your phone) to yourself describing where you want to be spiritually and what you hope is true of yourself and your relationship with God. Describe the kind of spiritual fruit you hope to grow in your life this year. Set a reminder to read it again in one year.

WEEK 10

VINE AND BRANCHES—TREE AND FRUIT

I am the true vine, and my Father is the gardener. He cuts off every branch in me that bears no fruit, while every branch that does bear fruit he prunes so that it will be even more fruitful. You are already clean because of the word I have spoken to you. Remain in me, as I also remain in you. No branch can bear fruit by itself; it must remain in the vine. Neither can you bear fruit unless you remain in me.

I AM THE VINE; YOU ARE THE BRANCHES.

If you remain in me and I in you, you will bear much fruit; apart from me you can do nothing. If you do not remain in me, you are like a branch that is thrown away and withers; such branches are picked up, thrown into the fire and burned. If you remain in me and my words remain in you, ask whatever you wish, and it will be done for you. This is to my Father's glory, that you bear much fruit, showing yourselves to be my disciples.

JOHN 15:1-8

No good tree bears bad fruit, nor does a bad tree bear good fruit.

Each tree is recognized by its own fruit. People do not pick figs from thorn bushes, or grapes from briers. A good man brings good things out of the good stored up in his heart, and an evil man brings evil things out of the evil stored up in his heart. For the mouth speaks what the heart is full of.

LUKE 6:43-45

FARMER

I remember reading John 15 for the first time. I was 19 years old. The thing that stuck out to me the most at that point in my life was that all the branches that don't bear fruit are cut off and thrown in the fire.

I had an idea of what that meant—knew it wasn't good—and knew it wasn't what I wanted.

I claimed to be a Christian. I was raised in church, after all. "Of course I believe in God," I told a friend. I'll get more serious when I get older. Following Jesus was something grown-ups did, I thought. When you're older, married, and have a family, that's when you settle down and become a boring, responsible adult who doesn't have any fun. This was the lie the enemy had tricked me into believing.

Looking back, my concept of being a Christian was weak. "Believing in God" (whatever that meant) and "going to church" (which hadn't been very interesting or special to me at that point).

A high school friend, who I grew up going to church with, started reaching out to me and asking honest questions like, *"Do you still believe in Jesus? Are you following Him? Where is there evidence or fruit in your life that you believe in God and know Him and love Him? How is He changing you? What are you learning in His Word?"*

The Lord used these questions to get the ball rolling in my mind and heart. **Never underestimate sincere questions and bold conversations!** These were the dominoes that started a chain reaction in my life. And though she may never read this—I'm eternally grateful to you, Julie!

I was stumped and taken aback. I wanted to be defensive, but I was exposed as the fraud I was. I was a plastic tree. Fake. Lifeless. Fruitless.

Being a true Christian means bearing real spiritual fruit. My branches were bare and for the first time, I saw it. I knew it and knew that it needed to change.

The idea of having a relationship with Jesus was foreign to me. But I could see it in the lives of some of my Christian peers. They actually loved Jesus. They didn't want or need the things I thought you needed to have fun and to have a good time. They wanted to spend time together talking about Jesus and reading the Bible and sharing what they were learning and getting stronger in their faith.

At the time—even though I had been raised in church—I didn't have a category for people "my age" choosing to get to know God without their parents "making them go to church." *You mean, people actually believe this and live like this??*

They were real. I was fake.

Not only did I not have genuine spiritual fruit to show, but the fruit I did have in my life was not good. The things that were coming out of my heart and my mouth were the opposite of good.

As men—if we want to be fruitful, life-giving farmers and providers—we have to possess what we profess. We have to be the real deal.

We have to be spiritually alive. We have to be actually, personally connected to Jesus.

Material and financial provision is important. Hard work and not being lazy is a big deal. But none of that matters if we're spiritually dead. You can do those other things and not even be spiritually alive.

Above and beyond those important material provisions and virtues, we are called to be the spiritual providers and spiritual leaders in our homes. We are called to be spiritually fruitful, and that means being a real tree, a good tree, a living branch, connected to the vine.

Men are doers. But before you're a *doer*, you have to be a *being*.

Look, I get it. Maybe you don't do the singing part and the emotional touchy-feely stuff. Not your cup of tea. I know a few guys who drink tea, but not many. Anyway. The whole conversation for a lot of guys about "abiding in Jesus" is weird.

Where's the action? Trust me, there's some action you don't want.

Like getting cut off and thrown in the fire. That is not the action you want.

Even the part about pruning—yeah, that's not going to be your favorite. It's painful at the time but productive in the end. Like the plow, we've got to embrace it.

Here's some of the good action that comes with being authentically connected to Jesus and producing real spiritual fruit:

- The action is found in being made a good tree that can actually bear good fruit and can speak life-giving words into the soul of your wife, children, friends, and even strangers.

- The action is in building a home of peace, where love and joy and laughter fill the air.

- The action is in knowing you're saved and going to spend eternity with Jesus and realizing that apart from Him, you're an absolute train wreck.

- The action is in living a life that glorifies God—where you experience personal fellowship with Jesus and the Holy Spirit and can't get enough.

- The action is in stacking God's Word in your heart and His Word abiding in you and changing the way you think, speak, and act.

- The action is in seeing the God of the universe answer your prayers.

- The action is in the transformation of your life and character into the image of Jesus over the course of your lifetime.

When you roll with Jesus, and you're about the Father's family farm, trust me, there's all the action you can imagine and then some.

If you think God is boring, I know one thing about you: you don't know Him yet.

When you learn to abide in Jesus and His words abide in you, life gets richer and sweeter. There's also a deeper sense of rest. Real rest. A sweeter, purer rest than you've ever known.

If you're honest, you know your soul needs rest. We need living, vital, abiding connection with Jesus.

> St. Augustine said, "You have made us for Yourself, O Lord, and our heart is restless until it finds its rest in Thee."

You need spiritual life flowing into you, like sap from a tree into its branches. From the roots up into the leaves.

Life. Juice. Energy.

Without Jesus, when you are living in your own strength, your soul is disconnected—you need to get plugged in.

Stronger men are men who know they constantly need Jesus.

"I am the vine; you are the branches."

"Apart from Me you can do nothing."

"Remain in Me as I also remain in you."

"You will know a tree by its fruit."

What kind of branch are you? Check the fruit.

FROM A STRONGER MAN

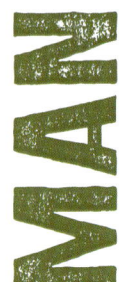

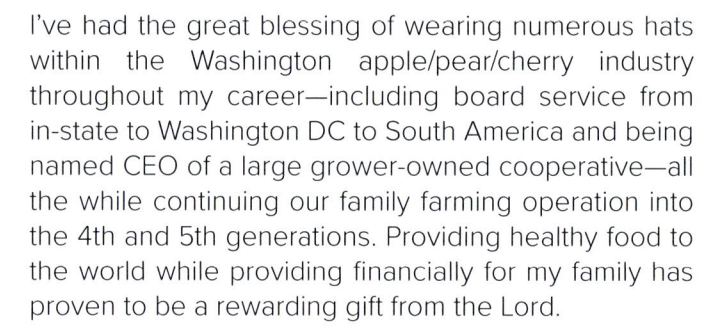

FARMER

I've had the great blessing of wearing numerous hats within the Washington apple/pear/cherry industry throughout my career—including board service from in-state to Washington DC to South America and being named CEO of a large grower-owned cooperative—all the while continuing our family farming operation into the 4th and 5th generations. Providing healthy food to the world while providing financially for my family has proven to be a rewarding gift from the Lord.

I've been walking with Jesus since an early age, led to the Lord by Jesus-loving parents and mentored by several SMN men. I've been married to my lovely wife for 17 years, and we are raising and praying for 4 children who are all loving and growing stronger in their faith in Jesus.

As I reflect on my experiences in farming, God has shown me that we live in a fallen, broken world; yet we hope that one day it will be made new. Think about it. Most of what farmers do is compensating for or fixing problems. Nutrient deficiencies that need corrected with inputs. Pest outbreaks that can wipe out an entire crop. Diseases that can decimate a farm and ultimately a farmer's livelihood—despite the best farming practices and being a diligent, hardworking farmer!

I've also learned that He is more concerned with my spiritual growth and character than a profit and loss statement or balance sheet. I've prayed earnestly during many a weather event—be it frost, hail, rain, excess heat, wind—and had the Lord remind me of Matthew 6 where He instructs us not to worry but trust that He will provide. He is the great Provider and has been proven faithful time and time again for our family for 5 generations.

In John 15, Jesus talks to the disciples about "The Vine and the Branches." mere hours before His arrest and crucifixion. I love that metaphor—Christ as the Vine and us as the branches. Apart from Him, we can do nothing. Removed from the vine, a branch will wither and bear no fruit. In this parable, He establishes Himself as Lord and speaks of Himself as the true vine, the One who will bear good fruit to reflect God's glory.

One of my favorite tasks in the fruit growing process is pruning. This is an annual task that involves total limb removal as well as shortening branches throughout the tree. It affects not only next year's crop but the shape and productivity of the trees for years to come. As a farmer, and specifically a tree fruit farmer, this passage from John 15 has always resonated with me. I've seen the results of pruning, both in the farming world and in my spiritual life. Jesus says in verse 2 that He will remove every branch that bears no fruit, while every branch that does bear fruit He prunes, so that it will be even more fruitful. Let's be men who willingly let the Vinedresser prune and shape us and our character. It'll bear much fruit for the Kingdom.

Mark, 41

REFLECT & DISCUSS

1. What is your biggest takeaway from this chapter?

2. How can you cultivate an ongoing connection with Jesus and His Word throughout the day?

3. What comes to mind when you think of "abiding" in Jesus? How can you strengthen or increase that connection in this season of your life?

4. What needs to be pruned from your life currently?

5. What are some examples of good fruit in your life in the last week? What are some examples of bad fruit?

_____

_____

_____

6. Over the course of your life, is there a time that stands out to you as the most "fruitless" time? How did God bring you through that time? What happened? What did you learn?

_____

_____

_____

7. What is your hope and desire for the spiritual fruitfulness of your family and what can you do this week to nurture and cultivate it?

_____

_____

_____

TAKE ACTION

- Focus on life-giving speech this week. "The mouth speaks what the heart is full of." Note the instances when the wrong thing(s) come out of your mouth. Note the instances when good things come out of your mouth. What did you learn?

- Find 2-3 additional verses in the Bible (use the concordance in the back of your Bible) that address the tongue or speech and note them here. Read them each day this week.

- Give specific verbal affirmations to your wife and kids each day this week. Make a list of 7 additional people in your life. Sincerely pray for them (focus specifically on one per day) and text each of them an encouraging text on the day you pray for them.

WEEK 11

STRONGER MEN ARE PATIENT FARMERS

Be patient, then, brothers, until the Lord's coming. See how the farmer waits for the land to yield its valuable crop and how patient he is for the autumn and spring rains.

YOU ALSO, BE PATIENT.

Establish your hearts, for the coming of the Lord is at hand.

JAMES 5:7-8

Farming requires patience. Something men are famous for...or maybe not so much.

All through Scripture and in nature, we see the need for patience as the farming and growing process unfolds. We plow, we plant, we water—and then, we wait!

James 5:7 says, "*Be patient, then, brothers, until the Lord's coming. See how the farmer waits for the land to yield its valuable crop and how patient he is for the autumn and spring rains.*"

How are you doing with patience?

Specifically, James is referring to the Lord's coming. But until then, there's a lot of patience needed for the trials, challenges, and mundane stuff of life we face, both small and big. And he has that in view, as well. Which is why he says one verse later, "Don't grumble against each other, brothers."

Many of the times we grumble are directly linked to impatience—just like the Israelites did in the wilderness after being saved out of Egypt.

In general, men aren't exactly known for possessing the quality of patience. In fact, true patience is itself a fruit of the Holy Spirit (Galatians 5:22). It's not natural, it's super-natural.

John Stott nailed it when he wrote, "The fruit of the Spirit take a lifetime to ripen." Perhaps especially patience.

Here are 6 truths about patience:

#1 PATIENCE IS NOT PASSIVITY.

When it comes to patience—while we wait to see growth, fruit, or change in our lives, in others, or in a situation—we must remember that patience is not the same as passivity.

If I'm honest, I often picture patience as a kind of weakness. It's soft. Weak. Passive. But that's absolutely false. Hard working farmers are patient but not passive. Stronger men are patient but not passive.

You can be passive (a vice) without being patient (a virtue), and you can be patient without being passive.

#2 PATIENCE IS ACTUALLY THE FRUIT OF INTENSE INTERNAL ACTION.

To become a patient man is to build significant internal fortitude of actively trusting, enduring, persevering, and long-suffering.

Patience is "the capacity to accept or tolerate delay, trouble, or suffering without getting angry or upset—self-restraint." Remaining calm and steadfast, forbearing in the face of trial, suffering, or delays.

That's the stuff of strength, not weakness.

Patience involves restraining the sinful flesh from acting out in anger or frustration, whereas passivity and weakness is giving in to the sinful flesh, giving up or giving in and no longer caring. No longer restraining.

#3 PATIENCE REMAINS ACTIVELY ENGAGED IN CHARACTER BUILDING.

Passivity checks out and disengages.

Consequently, it is a passive man who vents his anger unrighteously. It is a weak man who blusters and stomps and lets his tongue cut loose. A stronger man has the power to hold it back, step back, take a deep breath, and subdue the inner rampage.

We often think that patience is about waiting for things in our circumstances or situation to change. **But what if I told you that patience is less about a dramatic change in your circumstances and more about a dynamic, powerful process of change in your heart?** It takes the power of the Holy Spirit in you to be a truly patient man.

There are too many ripe examples to pick from when it comes to men and the lack of patience. See what I did there?

Consider the phenomena known as "family vacations." A 4-year-old boy was traveling with his parents and kept asking his mother, "Are we there yet?" "When are we going to get there?" Finally, the dad chimes in, rather irritated, "We have 200 miles to go, don't ask us when are we going to get there again! Wait until we get there, have some patience—sheesh!"

The boy is quiet for a while and then he timidly asks, "Mom, will I still be 4 when we get there?"

#4 PATIENCE DOESN'T COME NATURALLY.

It doesn't take many road trips with little kids to know that none of us were born with it. Not kids or parents.

Stop and think for a minute. How well do you wait:

- In traffic?
- When your son or daughter (or anyone) asks you the same question over and over again?
- When your son still hasn't taken out the garbage?
- When you're shopping with your wife?
- When your family is getting ready for that friend's wedding or event?

Just remember, you may feel like you wait too long at times for your wife and kids, but I'm going to give them the patience trophy, bro. They have to *live* with you.

Wanna hear something funny? As I've been writing this chapter, there has been a squirrel outside the window chirping non-stop. I've gotten up twice to throw ice chunks at it to try and get it to shut up.

God's sense of humor is amazing. A) God's beautiful creation singing His praise? Or, B) a demonic squirrel that needs to be cast into the lake? I'm saying (B).

Okay, where was I? Ah, yes, patience. *eye roll*

Let's consider a few more possible real-life scenarios in addition to the chirping squirrel:

- When that person at work is still talking?
- When you're waiting to hear back about that new job?
- When you're waiting for the market to bounce back?
- When the soonest doctor appointment is a month out?
- When you're waiting for the results?
- When you're waiting to hear that your daughter's plane safely landed?
- When you're waiting for an update to hear if your good friend or family member is okay after the accident?

Patience is indeed the stuff of spiritual strength. Thankfully, God is patient. And He judges time differently than we do.

We live in an age addicted to instant gratification. It's all about speed. From internet service to food service to travel. We are addicted to speed. No wonder why everyone is fried, frazzled, anxious, and angry.

WEEK ELEVEN

Boy, do we need farmers now more than ever.

#5 PATIENCE HAS PURPOSE.

The farmer knows that waiting, in God's economy, has a valuable reward. He knows that patience is not meaningless, useless, or in vain.

The farmer knows "important things are happening that you can't see."

We aren't just waiting for something to happen, things ARE happening. You just can't see them yet.

So what do you do?

James says, "establish your hearts." You need strength on the inside. Jesus patiently endured suffering and trusted His Father's plan while He waited. Through Him, you too can embrace the process that involves waiting even through pain, and remember that God is ultimately in charge.

There's a harvest being planned in and for your heart while you wait. Waiting is one of God's best tools that He uses to produce the sweet fruit of patience in you so that you can remain steadfast in trials and patient in affliction.

In the Christian life, we don't just wait for grace—waiting IS grace. God exposes something in us through it and promises to change us by it.

#6 PATIENCE ISN'T JUST WAITING FOR YOUR CIRCUMSTANCES TO CHANGE AS MUCH AS IT IS YOUR HEART CHANGING IN THE MIDST OF YOUR WAITING.

That's the way of patient farmers. The way of stronger men.

> Life on a farm is a school of patience; you can't hurry the crops or make an ox in two days.
>
> — Henri Alain

FROM A STRONGER MAN

After graduating from college, I spent 23 years in the grocery industry and my wife and I were owners for 17 of those years. The next 23 years were in the Ag (tree fruit & vineyards) industry. I spent 8 years as the office manager for a large independent orchard packing and storage operation. The next 15 years were spent with an Ag management and consulting company overseeing office activities and handling cash-flow management, including funding from independent growers, corporate farms, and pension funds.

In the 5th chapter of James, we are instructed to be patient until the Lord's coming. But how? We need to be transformed by the renewing of our mind. We can easily be patient when we anticipate a favorable outcome. It is more difficult to wait (be patient) when the outcome is unknown or something we definitely don't want to happen. The 3 Ts come to mind: trials, tribulation, trouble. The apostle Paul has a longer list in 2 Corinthians 11:23-27. I will just mention a few in his words: been in prison, been flogged, been exposed to death, pelted with stones, shipwrecked, and in danger from a variety of people. How did Paul handle all of his negative experiences? Not in his fleshly abilities.

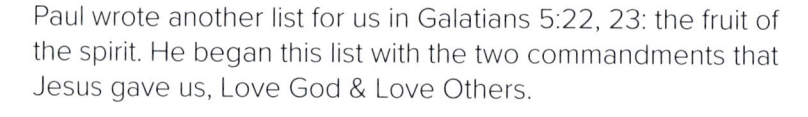

Paul wrote another list for us in Galatians 5:22, 23: the fruit of the spirit. He began this list with the two commandments that Jesus gave us, Love God & Love Others.

LOVE It embraces the whole list—the overall banner—it is grace.

JOY Constant delight in God. Nehemiah dealt with a lot of adversity, so he encouraged the stronger men of his day and in our time with the reminder, "the joy of the Lord is your strength."

PEACE Contentedness under pressure, while trusting God.

FORBEARANCE Being long-suffering.

KINDNESS & GOODNESS
These seem to overlap—being courteous, ready to help others, not self-centered.

FAITHFULNESS
To God (Hebrews 11:1) "Now faith is confidence in what we hope for and assurance about what we do not see."

GENTLENESS
Not quick to get angry—controlling our passions and resentments.

SELF-CONTROL
Not being excessive but sober-minded instead.

Trying harder in our flesh is not the answer. Waiting patiently is the Holy Spirit's doing as we submit to Him.

So how can we wait patiently as James stated and also accomplish it like Paul? I noticed recently that Paul always includes in his writing that he is continually thankful and grateful for God in his life.

It's a big deal when God calls us from death to life or from darkness to light. God always initiates. In our salvation and spiritual growth and gifting, God patiently waits. He has been waiting and will continue to wait patiently, as He conforms us to the image of His Son.

Larry, 76

REFLECT & DISCUSS

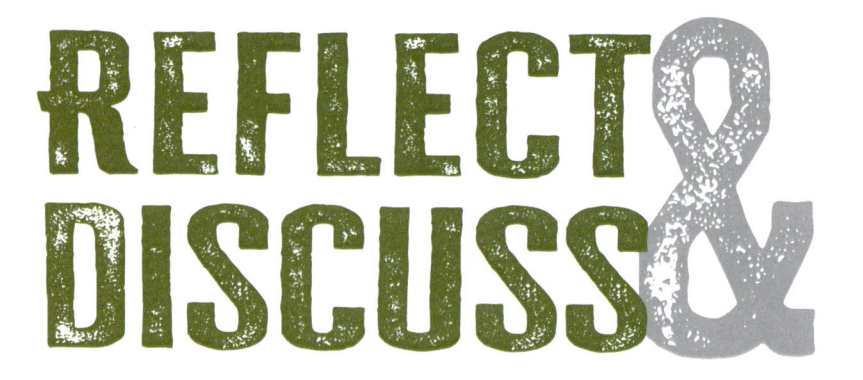

1. What is your biggest takeaway from this chapter?

2. What situations come to mind that regularly test your patience and expose your impatience?

3. When has/does grumbling show up in your life? What things do you find yourself grumbling about? How many of them are connected to a need for greater patience?

4. Which of the 6 truths about patience do you most need to remember this week and why?

WEEK ELEVEN

5. "Patience isn't just waiting for your circumstances to change as much as it is your heart changing in the midst of your waiting." Why is this a helpful perspective toward patience and how could this truth help you make progress in growing in patience?

_____
_____
_____

6. As you look at your life, in what ways has God been patient with you? Try and be as specific as possible.

_____
_____
_____

7. What encouraged you the most in this chapter? What challenged you the most?

_____
_____
_____

TAKE ACTION

- Make note this week of the times you experience impatience boiling up and over in your heart and responses. Repent of your impatience and ask God to help you in this area. Yes, men, I'm challenging you to pray for patience and then take your medicine like a man. :-)

- Find 2-3 additional specific Bible verses related to patience. Write them down and read over them each day this week.

- Make note of 2-3 specific situations this week in which you demonstrate the fruit of patience. Tell the men in your group or someone in your life about these experiences. Be encouraged—it's possible!

WEEK 12

ALL IN FOR THE LORD OF THE HARVEST

After this the Lord appointed seventy-two others and sent them two by two ahead of him to every town and place where he was about to go. He told them, **"The harvest is plentiful, but the workers are few.** Ask the Lord of the harvest, therefore, **to send out workers into his harvest field.** Go! I am sending you out like lambs among wolves. Do not take a purse or bag or sandals; and do not greet anyone on the road.

LUKE 10:1-4

"The harvest is plentiful, but the workers are few."

Welcome to the few. Stronger men are workers, committed to the harvest, because they are committed to the Lord of the harvest.

You get one life. How will you live it?

There are few things worse than realizing you gave it your all for the wrong reason in the wrong direction—on the wrong team for the wrong harvest.

Don't let the enemy beat you up or keep you down. God is still hiring. You can still go to work for Him. It's not too late. Now is the time. Don't waste another minute.

God can redeem the years the locusts have eaten. God can flip the script in your life and blow your mind with a harvest of impact through your repentance and a new testimony about a new mission.

The hour may be late. The time may be short. All the more, we need more hands on deck. More hands on more plows.

If you're a young person reading this, don't wait. Don't think you'll have time later. That, too, is a lie of the enemy. Start now. Start following Jesus now and start helping others meet, love, and follow Jesus.

Dads, raise your sons and daughters in the field. Raise them going after the harvest. Bring them with you. That's what your Heavenly Father wants to do with you.

Some workers come early, some workers come at midday, some workers come late in the day. God can use them all. He calls all of us to join Him in the field.

Young or old, spend the rest of your life—from this point forward—leveraging everything you have for the harvest. You'll never regret it.

What kind of harvest will your life produce? How will you help bring in the Lord's harvest?

It won't be easy. It won't be automatic. It won't be handed to you. You may even want to quit. But don't. Don't look back. Keep going. It'll be worth it.

As a young pastor friend of mine says, "It'll be greater later." We can work hard and persevere now because we pursue the harvest in hope of the celebration to come!

This is why just before saying, "the harvest is plentiful, but the workers are few," Jesus said, "No one who puts his hand to the plow and looks back is fit for service in the kingdom of God." (Luke 9:62)

You can start any time. You should start now. Just don't quit. Think it through, get started, and keep going.

Jesus is calling His men to be all in. Against all odds.

"Go! I'm sending you out like lambs among wolves."

Hard work. No turning back. Lambs among wolves. And yeah, the workers are few. But the harvest is plentiful. You in?

What a thrilling life!

"You mean, you can use me??"

"Yep. You. I'll use you. You can get in on this action. Let's go."

Let me clarify something. What is the harvest?

It's not what, it's who.

PEOPLE. The harvest is people.
Eternal souls. Thirsty. Hungry. Starving. Hurting. Dead in sin. Close to you but far from God—people.

Starting in your own house. And the house next door. And across the street. And in your class. On your team. At your work. At the store. And yes, around the world.

The harvest is plentiful, but they are "out there." We've got to go get it (them). Farm it. Harvest it. Bring it in.

This can be overwhelming for some. It's plentiful indeed! It's a big world. *Where do you start??*

Start right where you are.
Start with the low-hanging fruit.

Who's closest to you? Who do you know? Who's leaning in? Who do you know that needs Jesus? Who comes to mind? Who's open? Who's curious? Who's close?

Start there.

Imagine if we all did that, individually and collectively.

Just plow your row (those near you). Together, we can cover a lot of ground. Together, we can bring in more of the harvest than you can currently imagine.

Talk to a farmer and you'll quickly learn that everything they do—EVERYTHING—is for the harvest. The joy, the reward, the satisfaction, the "it-was-all-worth-it" feeling, is found in the harvest.

Being called into the harvest field by Jesus is an invitation into a life of joy. A life with a front row seat of God changing hearts and changing lives.

It's not about standing on a street corner. It's about building relationships. It's about loving people enough to tell them what Jesus has done in your life and helping them come to know and experience the same grace and truth.

In this week's passage in Luke 10, Jesus sends out 72 of His closest followers. 36 teams of two, hand-picked, sent out ahead with clear instructions.

Consider these insights and observations from this passage:

- We go in teams—there may be few, but we don't go alone.
- There's a sense of urgency—the harvest is ripe, now is the time.
- There are threats along the way.

- There are friends of the harvest and enemies of the harvest.
- We need more workers—pray for more workers, go make more workers.
- Don't get sidetracked.
- Don't get stuck, keep moving.
- Don't look back.
- Don't get deterred.
- Don't overcomplicate it.
- Don't let the enemy scare you.
- There is spiritual power available to those who go—you go in the power and authority of the Lord.
- Don't let it go to your head—stay humble.
- Don't rejoice that demons submit to you—rejoice that your names are written in heaven.
- Don't lose perspective—harvesting is the life of joy, a privilege and blessing to be used by God.
- Win the children—harvest the next generation.
- Jesus is on the move, and He's with us in the field.

Brothers, we are living in ripe days.

Stronger men are all in for one name. That name is Jesus Christ. And He's the Lord of the harvest.

The driving passion of a stronger man is a life lived for the glory of Jesus Christ. You get one life. How will you live it?

"The harvest is plentiful, but the workers are few. Ask the Lord of the harvest, therefore, to send out workers into his harvest field. Go! I am sending you out like lambs among wolves." —Jesus

FARMER

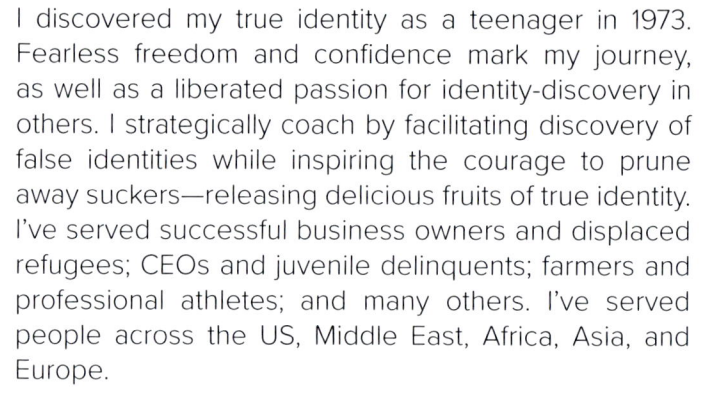

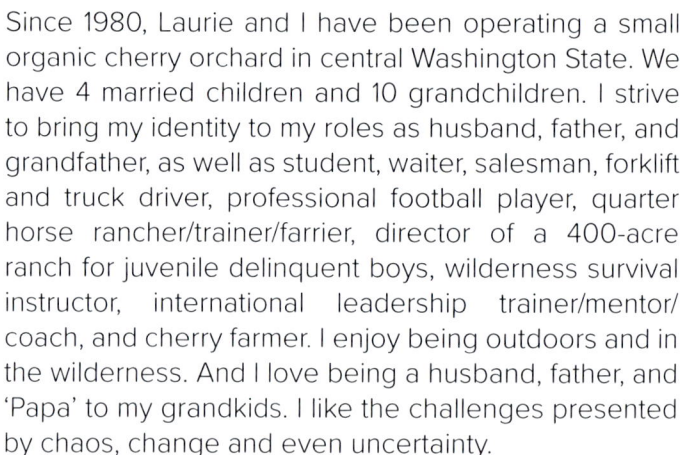

FROM A STRONGER MAN

I discovered my true identity as a teenager in 1973. Fearless freedom and confidence mark my journey, as well as a liberated passion for identity-discovery in others. I strategically coach by facilitating discovery of false identities while inspiring the courage to prune away suckers—releasing delicious fruits of true identity. I've served successful business owners and displaced refugees; CEOs and juvenile delinquents; farmers and professional athletes; and many others. I've served people across the US, Middle East, Africa, Asia, and Europe.

Since 1980, Laurie and I have been operating a small organic cherry orchard in central Washington State. We have 4 married children and 10 grandchildren. I strive to bring my identity to my roles as husband, father, and grandfather, as well as student, waiter, salesman, forklift and truck driver, professional football player, quarter horse rancher/trainer/farrier, director of a 400-acre ranch for juvenile delinquent boys, wilderness survival instructor, international leadership trainer/mentor/coach, and cherry farmer. I enjoy being outdoors and in the wilderness. And I love being a husband, father, and 'Papa' to my grandkids. I like the challenges presented by chaos, change and even uncertainty.

In cherry farming, every year we must prune the trees. They will not prune themselves. Every year, suckers grow in the tree. You can tell a sucker because it grows nice, beautiful leaves, sucks energy from the tree but produces no fruit. We cannot afford to take a year off from pruning our trees or the suckers take over. Same thing in our lives. God is a fruit lover, so let Him and those in your community help you prune. My mentor Rueben told me many years ago, "You have to hurt the trees; if you don't hurt the trees, no fruit!" Left on their own, cherry trees will grow wild, tall, full of suckers and useless for fruit.

Once the suckers are gone, the fruit-bearing branches are also lopped off so that energy is not used to grow the branch longer. All the nutrients are pushed back into the branch and used to produce delicious fruit. In

WEEK TWELVE

the tree, these fruit-bearing branches are never comparing themselves to one another. 'Why can't I be more like the other branches' is never heard or seen, because each fruit-bearing branch knows that the fruit is not coming from them. All the fruit comes from the direct relationship each branch has with the tree. Apart from the tree, the branch can produce nothing.

God is not mad at us for allowing the suckers in our lives to grow. He is the loving, tender Orchardist who loves His trees and faithfully wounds, cuts and nourishes each tree until it is producing the fruit it was created to produce. Let's get pruned, men. Let's endure the wounds that pruning our suckers will bring. The result will be real, lasting, tangible, and delicious fruit flowing from our relationship and connection with the Trinity.

It's harvest time, men! God wants you to be in it! Jesus said, "The harvest is plentiful but the workers are few." "Pray to the Lord of the harvest to send out more workers into the field."

Let Jesus prune away the lies of the enemy, those suckers in your life that are keeping you out of the harvest. No matter where you are or what you have done...Jesus prayed for you to join Him in the harvest. God loves you and He wants you to be with Him.

Norris, 65

REFLECT & DISCUSS

1. What is your biggest takeaway from this chapter?

2. Have you ever been involved in personally leading someone else to faith in Jesus? If yes, what was that like? If no, how strong is your desire to experience that in your life? What do you think that would be like?

3. What do you think you need to know, be, and/or do in order to be more prepared and equipped to be an effective worker in the harvest? What's your next step? Who could you talk to about these things?

4. What are some of the hurdles or fears that you have when it comes to sharing Jesus with others? What gets in the way or holds you back?

WEEK TWELVE

5. What are some of the reasons in this passage (Luke 10:1-4) that Christians should have confidence and courage to share Christ with others?

6. In the bulleted list of insights/observations from Luke 10, which ones stand out to you or resonate most with you and why?

7. Who are some of the people in your life that you could go with as you head out into the harvest field? Who could you potentially partner up with?

TAKE ACTION

- Take 3 minutes to think and pray quietly, asking the Lord to show you who in your life or around you might be ripe/open to the gospel. Write down a list of names that come to mind and begin praying for them each day this week. Watch for opportunities to interact or connect with them. What would be a next step you could take in relationship or conversation with them? Make a plan to follow through.

- Ask God to bring some names to mind of people you could partner with in sharing Christ with others (through starting a small group or hosting a bbq or intentionally planning a social event to help build or strengthen relationship with someone who needs Jesus). Write down those potential mission/harvest partner names. Reach out to them this week to see if they are open to exploring some intentional harvest partnership with you.

(Continued on next page...)

TAKE ACTION
(CONTINUED)

- Write out a 15-second version of your personal testimony of faith in Jesus to prepare to share with others. Here's a simple template to use:

    1. "There was a time in my life when I was _____ & _____, …"

    (List two characteristics about your life before knowing Jesus. Ex "broken" "lost" "selfish" "scared" "trapped" "uncertain" "hopeless". Use words that are personal to your story).

    2. "But then Jesus saved me and I began to follow Him. Since then, my life is now filled with _____ & _____."

    (List two characteristics about your life since coming to know and follow Jesus. Ex. "hope" "joy" "love" "purpose" "security" "peace" "freedom". Use words that are personal to your story).

    3. "Do you have a story like that?"

    (This is a simple question you can use in conversation with someone after you have an opportunity to share your short testimony).

> So neither he who plants nor he who waters is anything, but only God who gives the growth. He who plants and he who waters are one, and each will receive his wages according to his labor. For we are God's fellow workers. You are God's field, God's building.
>
> — 1 Corinthians 3:7-9

ADDITIONAL QUESTIONS FOR DISCUSSION

1. What's the best job you've ever had? What's the worst?

2. For fun/hypothetically: If you could do something entirely different career-wise, what would it be and why?

3. Describe your all-time ideal Saturday for each season: fall, winter, spring, summer.

4. What's the best trip you've ever taken?

5. If you could travel anywhere in the world—where would it be and why?

6. Who were your heroes growing up? Who are your heroes today?

7. In what ways would you want to emulate attributes and qualities of manhood from your father?

8. In what ways would you NOT want to emulate attributes and qualities of manhood from your father?

9. How would you describe the kind of legacy you want to leave? What words do you hope others use to describe your impact?

10. Share a version of your spiritual history and journey.

11. What were your first experiences of church like?

12. What would you say is the biggest current hurdle or obstacle in your life?

13. What weighs on your mind/heart the most these days?

14. What changes are needed in your current family routine (daily, weekly, monthly)?

15. What do you do for fun? What do you do with your family for fun?

16. Are you satisfied with your current level of availability and connection with your wife and kids? What would improve it?

17. Are you satisfied with your current relationship with God? What would improve it?

18. If you could meet and spend an hour with anyone in history—who would it be and why? Who would be in your Top 5.

19. What current living leader would you most want to spend a day shadowing and why?

20. If you could talk to your 18-year-old self, what would you say? What counsel/advice would you give yourself? (To a young man reading this: What advice would you give yourself 2 years ago?)

WAYS TO PRACTICE BEING A FARMER / PROVIDER

- Work Hard.

- Have a vision for your life.

- Know who you are and what you're about - know your core values.

- Have a plan for what you will do, where you will live, how you will provide for yourself and others.

- Earn money honestly.

- Steward money carefully.

- Spend money cautiously.

- Save money steadily.

- Invest money wisely.

- Give money generously.

- Have an emergency fund in place.

- Have good health insurance and life insurance in place.

- Think about the possibility of your early/untimely death and plan accordingly so your wife and family is well cared for.

- Have a plan for emergencies...like a house fire, flood, extended power outage, food shortage.

- Have a supply of freeze-dried food.

- Learn basic survival skills like shelter building and hunting/food creation.

- Learn how to build and fix useful items around the house, like furniture, basic home repair, plumbing, electrical, sheetrock, hvac, painting, flooring.

- Grow a garden.

- Raise farm animals.

- Live in life-giving relationships and community with others where certain items can be shared, swapped, handed down. (ie kids clothes, tools, equipment)

- Read the Bible to your family.

- Pray with and for your family.

- Take your family to church.

- Listen carefully to your wife and kids…listening for their emotional needs.

- Verbally affirm your wife and children—providing emotional strength.

- Show proper physical touch to your wife and children, providing emotional security and stability.

A final word of hope…

THE STRONGER MAN, JESUS CHRIST, WILL RESTORE THE GARDEN

Then the angel showed me the river of the water of life, as clear as crystal, flowing from the throne of God and of the Lamb down the middle of the great street of the city. **On each side of the river stood the tree of life, bearing twelve crops of fruit, yielding its fruit every month. And the leaves of the tree are for the healing of the nations. No longer will there be any curse.** The throne of God and of the Lamb will be in the city, and his servants will serve him. They will see his face, and his name will be on their foreheads. There will be no more night. They will not need the light of a lamp or the light of the sun, for the Lord God will give them light. And they will reign for ever and ever.

REVELATION 22:1-5

Come to me, all you who are weary and burdened, and I will give you rest. Take my yoke upon you and learn from me, for I am gentle and humble in heart, and you will find rest for your souls. For my yoke is easy and my burden is light.

— Jesus (Matthew 11:28-30)